AIR CAMPAIGN

PHILIPPINES 1944

Third Fleet's first victory over Japanese land-based airpower

EDWARD M. YOUNG | ILLUSTRATED BY JIM LAURIER

OSPREY PUBLISHING
Bloomsbury Publishing Plc
Kemp House, Chawley Park, Cumnor Hill, Oxford OX2 9PH, UK
29 Earlsfort Terrace, Dublin 2, Ireland
1385 Broadway, 5th Floor, New York, NY 10018, USA
E-mail: info@ospreypublishing.com
www.ospreypublishing.com

OSPREY is a trademark of Osprey Publishing Ltd

First published in Great Britain in 2024

© Osprey Publishing Ltd, 2024

All rights reserved. No part of this publication may be reproduced or transmitted in any form or by any means, electronic or mechanical, including photocopying, recording, or any information storage or retrieval system, without prior permission in writing from the publishers.

A catalog record for this book is available from the British Library.

ISBN: PB 9781472860439; eBook 9781472860446; ePDF 9781472860415; XML 9781472860422

Maps and diagrams by www.bounford.com
3D BEVs by Paul Kime
Index by Zoe Ross
Typeset by PDQ Digital Media Solutions, Bungay, UK
Printed by Repro India Ltd.

Title page: See page 67.

Osprey Publishing supports the Woodland Trust, the UK's leading woodland conservation charity.

To find out more about our authors and books visit www.ospreypublishing.com. Here you will find extracts, author interviews, details of forthcoming events and the option to sign up for our newsletter.

AIR CAMPAIGN

CONTENTS

INTRODUCTION	4
CHRONOLOGY	9
ATTACKER'S CAPABILITIES	11
DEFENDER'S CAPABILITIES	28
CAMPAIGN OBJECTIVES	40
THE CAMPAIGN	45
ANALYSIS AND CONCLUSION	90
FURTHER READING	94
INDEX	95

INTRODUCTION

US Navy LSTs unloading troops and supplies at Tanamerah Bay, near Hollandia, New Guinea. General Douglas MacArthur's forces landed near Hollandia on April 22, 1944. The successful capture of the area forced the Japanese to establish a new defensive line to the west and brought Allied forces closer to the approach to the Philippines. (80G-251402, Record Group 80, National Archives and Records Administration (NARA))

In September 1944, the US Navy's Fast Carrier Task Force carried out a series of strikes against Japanese forces in the Philippines. This was the first time that the Navy's carriers had conducted a sustained attack not on an isolated island air base but on a land mass that allowed defense in depth with aircraft deployed over many coordinated airfields spread across the Philippines. The aim was to destroy Japanese land-based air power in the Philippines and inflict the maximum possible damage against Japanese shipping. During the interwar years, it was thought that a carrier force would have difficulty overcoming land-based air power because land-based aircraft would likely be available in greater numbers than the carriers could deploy and could operate from a network of airbases that carriers would be unlikely to destroy in their entirety. Carrier aircraft might temporarily incapacitate an airfield on land, but a single heavy bomb could eliminate a carrier. The sinking of the *Prince of Wales* and the *Repulse* off the coast of Malaya at the start of the Pacific War underlined the risk of surface ships operating within the range of land-based air power, but by the summer of 1944 the US Navy had demonstrated its ability to destroy Japanese air power on isolated islands in the Central Pacific, and, in the battle for the Marianas, to sustain an attack for some time while defending its carrier force against counterattacks. But the Fast Carrier Task Force had yet to attempt an attack on a large land mass holding considerable numbers of enemy aircraft.

Following the successful American invasion of the Marianas in June 1944, the Japanese and American high commands both faced a strategic crossroads. For the Japanese, the issues were how to prepare for the inevitable next stage of the American advance towards Japan, and where this advance was most likely to occur. For the Americans, the debate focused on choosing the best route to defeat Japan among several different options. By early September, the Japanese and the Americans had made their choices. The Imperial Japanese Army and Navy were actively preparing for what was expected to be a decisive battle in one of four probable areas of an American attack. The American Joint Chiefs of Staff had agreed on a plan to continue the advance across the Pacific to the southern Philippines, leaving open the question of objectives for further advances towards Japan. One outcome of American

US Marine Corps LVTs head to the beaches on Saipan on June 15, 1944. The invasion and loss of the Marianas was an even more devastating blow to Japan's defensive strategy. (USMC 81842, Navy History and Heritage Command (NHHC))

deliberations was an order for Task Force 38, as the Navy's Fast Carrier Task Force was designated under the command of Admiral William Halsey, to carry out a series of strikes against the Philippines in September. The September raids demonstrated the striking power of US Navy carrier-based air power. Catching the Imperial Army and Navy forces in the Philippines before they had completed their reorganization and re-equipment, the apparent weakness of the Japanese response led to the Joint Chiefs of Staff cancelling planned landings on Mindanao and accelerating the date of landings on Leyte.

Japan's shrinking defensive barrier

Japan's strategy in the Pacific War was to establish a defensive barrier around the areas captured in Japan's initial offensive and to defeat American efforts to penetrate this barrier until America was exhausted. Following the Japanese defeat and withdrawal from Guadalcanal in February 1943, Japan's Imperial General Headquarters ordered a shift from offensive to defensive operations. Japan's first line of defense would stretch from the Aleutians to the Marshall and Gilbert Islands in the Central Pacific to the central Solomons. The Allies, however, now had the initiative and progressively broke through Japan's first defensive line, moving up the Solomon Islands toward the key Japanese base at Rabaul on New Britain, defeating Japanese forces in eastern New Guinea, and capturing positions in the Gilbert and the Marshall Islands. Excessive losses and growing Allied air superiority forced the Imperial Navy to withdraw its aircraft from Rabaul while carrier strikes in February severely damaged the Imperial Navy's base at Truk, limiting its effectiveness. By April 1944, Japan had established a new absolute line of defense that now went from the Marianas to Truk to Biak off the coast of western New Guinea. This line was to be held at all costs. The Imperial Navy made plans to utilize the Combined Fleet in a decisive battle against the American Navy in the seas west of the Marianas or around the Carolines in Operation *A-Go*.

By this point in the war the preponderance of air, military, and naval strength was decidedly in favor of the Allies. During April, Allied forces captured the Admiralty Islands, completing the isolation of Rabaul, and landed at Hollandia, making Japanese positions in eastern New Guinea untenable. A month later American forces landed on Biak, breaking the southern point of Japan's defensive line and giving the Americans a base for extending control over the approaches to the southern Philippines. Then, on June 15, the Americans landed on Saipan following carrier strikes. The American invasion triggered the *A-Go* operation, resulting in a devastating loss to the Imperial Navy's Combined Fleet and land-based air power in the Battle of the Philippine Sea. In two days of combat, the American Task Force 58 destroyed over 500 Japanese naval aircraft and sank two fleet carriers and one light carrier. The trained Imperial Navy air crews lost in the battle were irreplaceable. The loss of the Marianas placed American forces within 1,500 miles of the Home Islands of Japan, well within the range of the new Boeing B-29 long-range bombers, and gave the Fast Carrier Task Force supremacy over the Western Pacific. The public announcement of the loss of Saipan on July 18 forced General Tojo Hideki to resign as Prime Minister, Minister of War, and Chief of the Army General Staff, together with his entire cabinet.

Japan now had to fall back on its inner line of defense running from the Kurile Islands in the north and the Home Islands to the Ryukyus, Formosa (now Taiwan), and the Philippines to the Netherlands East Indies. Defense of the Philippines now became of vital importance to the defense of the Empire. Loss of the Philippines would sever Japan's connection with the fuel and raw materials in Southeast Asia critical to Japan's military industry, and provide a base for an American assault on the Home Islands. While recognizing the possibility that the Americans could advance directly against Japan through the Central Pacific, Imperial General Headquarters considered it more likely that the American advances through the Central and Southwest Pacific would converge on the Philippines, to provide bases for land-based air power to cover operations against Formosa and the Ryukyus. In late July, Imperial General Headquarters issued plans to the Imperial Army and Navy to prepare for decisive battles against the four likely areas of advance. This was designated *Sho-Go*, or Victory Operation, as follows:

Sho Operation No. 1: action against the Philippines.
Sho Operation No. 2: action against Formosa and the Ryukyu Islands.
Sho Operation No. 3: action against the Japanese Home Islands.
Sho Operation No. 4: action against the Kuriles and Hokkaido.

Imperial General Headquarters allocated forces to defend each of these areas and created plans for their employment, designating some to commit all their strength to an attack in their area, to send some or all forces to another area under attack, or act as a reserve. Once the area of the American advance had been determined, Imperial General Headquarters would initiate the respective *Sho* operation. Imperial General Headquarters gave priority in defensive preparations for the *Sho* operation to the Philippines, and Japanese forces in the islands had to be made ready to destroy an American attack.

Choosing the best route to Japan

War Plan Orange, the American military's prewar plan for a war against Japan, envisioned a war in three phases: in Phase I, Japanese forces would capture American possessions in the Pacific and seize oil and other resources in Southeast Asia; in Phase II, American naval and air forces would move westward across the Pacific, capturing some Japanese bases and bypassing others in a war of attrition that would include regaining a base in the Philippines; in Phase III, American forces would capture bases closer to Japan, cutting off the flow of vital raw materials and bombarding Japanese cities until Japan was forced to surrender. War Plan Orange did not foresee intensive combat against Japanese forces in the South Pacific, the need to insure the line of communications between America and Australia, or the possibility that America might become simultaneously involved in a major war in Europe. During 1942, events in the Pacific diverged from the underlying premise of War Plan Orange.

Following General Douglas MacArthur's withdrawal from the Philippines, at the end of March 1942 President Franklin Roosevelt approved a divided command for the Pacific. MacArthur was appointed Supreme Allied Commander for the Southwest Pacific covering Australia, New Guinea, and the Netherlands East Indies. Admiral Chester Nimitz, Commander in Chief of the Pacific Fleet, was made Commander in Chief, Pacific Ocean Area, covering the Central and South Pacific.

Over the next year and a half Allied forces stopped Japanese offensives in the Solomon Islands and New Guinea, and took the initiative. MacArthur's American and Australian air and ground forces pushed the Japanese back in eastern New Guinea while airmen, sailors, and troops under Admiral William Halsey's South Pacific Area command slowly moved up the Solomon Islands chain towards Rabaul on New Britain. Admiral Nimitz began the Central Pacific offensive in November 1943 with the invasion and capture of the Gilbert Islands. The American Joint Chiefs of Staff (JCS) had determined that, even with the priority placed on defeating Germany before Japan, America had the industrial capacity to support two separate drives across the Pacific. This gave America more offensive flexibility, confused the Japanese high command, and more rapidly wore down Japanese forces in the battle of attrition assigned to Phase II of War Plan Orange. By March 1944 it was clear that Nimitz's Central Pacific offensive and MacArthur's Southwest Pacific offensive were converging on the Philippines. How, where, when, and to what extent American forces should re-enter the Philippines became the subject of intense debate.

The American and British Combined Chiefs of Staff had agreed that the main offensive against Japan would be through the Pacific and not from Southeast Asia or China.

General Douglas MacArthur and Admiral Chester Nimitz presented their plans for continuing their offensives to President Franklin Roosevelt at a meeting at Pearl Harbor in July 1944. Left to right, MacArthur, Admiral William Leahy, President Roosevelt, and Admiral Nimitz. (80G-46221, RG80, NARA)

The JCS believed it would be important to seize a foothold in the Philippines, but as a base for further operations against Luzon or Formosa that could serve as bases for the invasion of Japan. In March 1944 the JCS ordered MacArthur to prepare plans to capture Mindanao with landings on November 15, 1944. General MacArthur believed that America had a moral obligation to liberate the Philippine people from Japanese occupation and that there were sound strategic reasons for capturing all of the Philippines. He wanted to use Mindanao as a base to advance to Luzon He proposed seizing Leyte in the central Philippines after the capture of Mindanao to build bases for land-based air power that could reduce Japanese air forces in Luzon prior to an invasion.

Admiral Nimitz and Admiral Ernest J. King, Chief of Naval Operations, while agreeing on the need to capture Mindanao, argued for bypassing Luzon in favor of capturing Formosa, which they thought would provide a better base for launching an invasion of Japan. The difficulty was that the forces available for an invasion of Formosa were deemed to be insufficient to what would be required. Additional forces might become available if the war against Germany ended in 1944, but in August 1944 that could not be taken as a certainty. At the end of August, MacArthur submitted a new timetable for the Southwest Pacific offensive, proposing landings on Morotai on September 15 to coincide with the Central Pacific Area's planned landings in Palau, a landing on the southernmost tip of Mindanao on November 15, a landing on Leyte on December 20, and a possible landing on Luzon on February 20, 1945. Unable to get the Army's agreement to invade Formosa, the Navy reluctantly accepted MacArthur's plan for invading Leyte. Leyte at least would provide bases, depots, and a fleet anchorage for a future advance on Formosa or directly to Japan. The JCS decided to defer a decision on invading Luzon or Formosa and instead, on September 8, 1944, ordered MacArthur to invade Leyte on December 20, 1944, with Admiral Nimitz providing the Fast Carrier Task Force in support of the landings.

CHRONOLOGY

1944

January 31 Marines and Army troops land on Kwajalein and Majuro in the Marshall Islands.

February Japanese withdraw all aircraft from Rabaul.

February 16–17 Task Force 58 carries out Operation *Hailstone*, the attack on the Japanese base at Truk.

February 22 Task Force 58 conducts the first strike on the Marianas.

February 29 Landings begin on the Admiralty Islands.

March 30 Task Force 58 attacks airfields and shipping in the Caroline Islands.

April 22 Allied forces land at Hollandia.

May 27 American forces land on Biak.

June 6 Capture of Hollandia completed.

June 11 TF58 launches attacks on Japanese airfields in the Marianas.

June 12–14 TF58 continues strikes against Saipan, Tinian, and Guam.

June 15 Operation *Forager* begins with US Marines landing on Saipan.

June 19 Battle of the Philippine Sea begins, TF58 claims more than 350 Japanese aircraft shot down.

June 20 Battle of the Philippine Sea concludes with heavy losses to Imperial Japanese Navy aircraft and fleet.

July 4 TG58.1 and TG58.2 strike Iwo Jima and Chichi Jima.

July 9 Capture of Saipan completed.

July 6–14 TF58 carries out strikes on Guam.

July 18 Field Marshal Tojo Hideki and his cabinet forced to resign over loss of Saipan.

July 21 Guam invaded.

July 24 Imperial Army and Navy agree on air operations plan for *Sho-Go*, the Victory Operation.

In September 1944 Task Force 38 contained six Essex-class fleet carriers, each carrying upwards of a hundred aircraft, creating a powerful striking force that could range across the Pacific, almost with impunity. Here VB-15 Curtiss Helldivers crowd the deck of USS *Essex* a month after the September strikes on the Philippines. (80G-258185, RG80, NARA)

July 25 TG58.1 strikes the Palau Islands.

July 26–28 President Roosevelt meets with General MacArthur and Admiral Nimitz in Pearl Harbor to discuss American strategy for the Pacific.

August 4–5 TG58.1, TG58.2, and TG58.3 attack Iwo, Chichi, and Haha Jima.

August 18 Vice Admiral John McCain relieves Rear Admiral J. J. Clark as Commander TG58.1.

August 26 Admiral William Halsey, Commander Third Fleet, relieves Admiral Spruance. Task Force 58 becomes Task Force 38, Task Groups 58.1, 58.2, 58.3, and 58.4 become Task Groups 38.1, 38.2, 38.3, and 38.4.

August 28 Admiral Halsey and TF38 sortie from Eniwetok.

August 31–September 2 TG38.4 conducts strikes against Iwo and Chichi Jima.

September 6–8 TG38.1, 38.2, and 38.3 launch strikes against Palau Islands prior to invasion.

September 8 American Joint Chiefs of Staff set November 15 as date for invasion of Mindanao; December 20 for invasion of Leyte.

September 9–10 Leaving TG38.4 off Palau, Admiral Halsey and TG38.1, 38.2, and 38.3 launch strikes against airfields and shipping at Mindanao.

September 12–14 TF38 strikes the Visayan Islands, concentrating on Cebu and Negros.

September 13 TG38.1 detached to support landings on Morotai scheduled for September 15.

September 13 Based on weak Japanese response to his carrier strikes, Admiral Halsey recommends to Nimitz cancelling invasion of Mindanao and advancing date of Leyte invasion to October 20.

September 14 Admiral Nimitz and General MacArthur submit Halsey's recommendations to the Combined Chiefs of Staff meeting in Quebec. The CCS take 90 minutes to give their approval.

September 14 TG38.2 and 38.3 strike Panay Island and Negros Island in the Visayas.

September 21 TG38.1, 38.2, and 38.3 strike airfields on Luzon, hitting Nichols Field and Clark Field, and attacking shipping in Manila Bay

September 22 Strikes continue around Luzon, hitting Japanese shipping in Manila Bay. Japanese planes attack TG38.1 and 38.3.

September 24 Final Philippine strikes target the Visayan Islands, TG38.1 and 38.2 attack shipping at Coron Bay off Calamian Island.

The TBF/TBM Avenger served in the torpedo squadrons (VT) aboard Essex-class and Independence-class carriers. By now most VT squadrons, including VT-18 shown here, flew the TBM-1C version built by the General Motors Corporation. The Avenger could carry a variety of weapons, including HVAR rockets under the wings. (80G-244804, RG80, NARA)

ATTACKER'S CAPABILITIES
The Fast Carrier Task Force

Commanders

After a year in combat, the Fast Carrier Task Force benefited from having capable commanders at all levels, many now with combat experience. Shortly before the September carrier strikes on the Philippines, the Navy instituted several changes in command. With the prospect of intensive and sustained operations against Japan as the Fast Carrier Task Force continued its advance across the Pacific, in May 1944 Admiral Nimitz and Admiral King introduced a two-platoon system whereby while one fleet commander and his staff carried out operations, the other fleet commander and his staff would be planning the next. Admiral Raymond Spruance was then commanding the Central Pacific Force, including the Fast Carrier Task Force designated Task Force 58 under Vice Admiral Marc Mitscher. At the end of April 1944, Spruance was appointed commander of the Fifth Fleet, he, his staff, and Mitscher and his staff, forming one of Nimitz's two command platoons. To alternate with Spruance, Nimitz and King chose Admiral William Halsey, commander of the South Pacific Area and the US Navy's Third Fleet. With the Solomon campaign completed, the South Pacific Area was to be downgraded, freeing Halsey for a new assignment. Halsey took his fleet command to Pearl Harbor and the Central Pacific Area. Under Halsey's command the Fast Carrier Task Force would become Task Force 38.

William Halsey had become an aviator in 1935 at the age of 52, the oldest aviation cadet in US Navy history. At the start of the war Halsey commanded USS *Enterprise* and participated in the first US Navy carrier strikes against the Japanese in the Pacific. He took command of the South Pacific Area in October 1942 in the midst of the desperate battle for Guadalcanal, and remained in command during the advance north up the Solomon Island chain. Halsey was not strong on administration, but he was an aggressive and popular commander, winning renown as "Bull" Halsey. While Halsey had commanded carriers and had carriers assigned to his Third Fleet command, he had not yet commanded a carrier task force. Halsey relieved Admiral Spruance on August 26, 1944.

12 ATTACKER'S CAPABILITIES

Vice Admiral John McCain, left, in conversation with Admiral William Halsey in December 1944. Aggressive and sometimes impulsive, Halsey took command over the Fast Carrier Task Force in August 1944 as Task Force 38, while McCain took command of Task Group 38.1 to gain experience with the fast carriers. (80G-302244, RG80, NARA)

To replace Mitscher in command of the Fast Carrier Task Force under Halsey, Admiral King selected Vice Admiral John McCain. Like Halsey a graduate of the US Naval Academy McCain also, like Halsey, qualified as a pilot in 1935. At the start of the war McCain was commander of Scouting Force, Atlantic Fleet, but in May 1942 was given command of all land-based aircraft in the South Pacific. He held this command until October when he became head of the Bureau of Aeronautics, becoming Deputy Chief of Naval Operations (Air) in August 1943. McCain had no experience commanding carriers. To give him an opportunity to learn, McCain assumed command of Task Group 38.1 in August 1944.

After the Marianas battle there were several changes in Task Group commands. Rear Admiral J. J. "Jocko" Clark, who had commanded USS *Yorktown*, remained with TG38.1 to support Admiral McCain. Rear Admiral Frederick C. Sherman had become a naval aviator in the mid-1930s like Halsey and McCain. Known as fearless, a hard taskmaster, and a superb tactician, Sherman had commanded carriers and carrier groups almost continuously since the beginning of the war. After a short shore posting he returned to the fast carriers in August 1944 to take command of Task Group 38.3.

Two younger commanders, both from the Naval Academy class of 1916 and experienced aviators, took over the other two Task Groups in Task Force 38. Rear Admiral Ralph Davison had been on the staff of the Bureau of Aeronautics during 1942–43, but took command of an escort carrier group in November 1943, participating in the invasions of the Marshall

Rear Admiral Frederick Sherman, who had extensive experience commanding carriers since the beginning of the war, returned to the fast carriers in August 1944 to take command of Task Group 38.3 just before the strikes against the Philippines. (80G-44090, RG80, NARA)

Islands and Hollandia in 1944. He was the first of the escort carrier group commanders to move up to the fleet carriers, taking command of Task Group 38.4. Davison's classmate Rear Admiral Gerald Bogan followed a similar route to task group command. Bogan had commanded USS *Saratoga* during 1942–43 and took command of an escort carrier group in January 1944, supporting invasion forces in the Pacific. His performance as an escort group commander won him promotion to the fast carriers. In August, Admiral Nimitz assigned Bogan to command Task Group 38.2.

The carrier and air group commanders in Task Force 38 were all experienced naval officers. The carrier captains had graduated from the US Naval Academy after World War I and had spent years as naval aviators. During the summer of 1944, several "fleeted-up" to the fast carriers after commanding escort carriers. Capt Oscar Weller took command of USS *Wasp* (CV-18) in July after commanding USS *White Plains* (CVE-66) in the Pacific; Capt Austin Doyle went to USS *Hornet* (CV-12) in August having commanded USS *Nassau* (CVE-16); while that same month Capt Marshall Greer took over command of USS *Bunker Hill* (CV-17) after spending nearly a year as captain of USS *Core* (CVE-13) in the Atlantic, the *Core* claiming two U-boats while under his command.

A naval aviator since 1925, Rear Admiral Gerald Bogan commanded USS *Saratoga* early in the war. His performance as a commander of an escort carrier group in the Pacific in the first half of 1944 earned him a promotion to command Task Group 38.2. (80G-468909, RG80, NARA)

The carrier air group commanders (CAG) were from a younger generation of Naval Academy graduates, typically completing their aviation training in the mid-1930s. They brought to their commands varied flying experience. Cdr Jackson Arnold, commanding Air Group 2 on the *Hornet*, had flown floatplanes off a cruiser, served as an engineering test pilot, and commissioned VT-2 and led the squadron into combat before becoming Air Group 2's commander. Cdr Ralph Shipley, CAG of Air Group 8 on the *Bunker Hill*, had been an instructor at Naval Air Station Jacksonville before taking command of VB-8 in 1943. Cdr David McCampbell, who became the Navy's top ace in World War II, had trained as a fighter pilot, served as the Landing Signals Officer on USS *Wasp*, and was also a flying instructor at NAS Jacksonville, commissioned VF-15 which he led until his promotion to Air Group 15 commander in February 1944. Arnold, Shipley, and McCampbell are representative of the air group commanders in Task Force 38 who led and coordinated the air strikes on the Philippines in September 1944.

Carriers and air groups

The US Navy relied principally on two classes of aircraft carriers to make up the Fast Carrier Task Force, the large Essex-class fleet carriers (designated CV) and the smaller Independence-class light carriers (designated CVL) (two earlier carriers USS *Saratoga* (CV-3) and USS *Enterprise* (CV-6) also served). The differences between the two classes were size and aircraft complement. Design of USS *Essex* (CV-9), the first of its class, began in 1939 building on the earlier Yorktown class and USS *Hornet* (CV-8). US Navy carrier doctrine emphasized offensive capacity over protective measures. The Essex class was designed to carry the maximum number of aircraft. An armored flight deck creates structural and weight issues that can reduce aircraft carrying capacity, but in an Essex-class carrier the hangar deck was

ATTACKER'S CAPABILITIES

The "wheels" of Carrier Air Group 2 in the summer of 1944. These men are representative of the capable and experienced commanders at the tactical level in Task Force 38. Left to right, Lt Cdr L.M.D. Ford, CO VT-2; Lt Cdr G.B. Campbell, CO VB-2; Capt W.D. Sample, CO USS *Hornet*; Lt Cdr W.A. Dean, CO VF-2; Cdr R. Johnson, *Hornet* Air Officer. (80G-367281, RG80, NARA)

USS *Essex* (CV-9), seen here in 1943 with a deck load of SBD Dauntless dive bombers, TBF Avengers, and F6F Hellcats, was the first in its class of large fleet carriers that became the backbone of the Fast Carrier Task Force. Admiral Halsey would take six of these large carriers to the Philippines in September 1944. (80G-68097, RG80, NARA)

the main strength deck and was made of armored steel. The 862ft by 108ft flight deck was made of sheet steel and covered in three-inch thick teak planks. Two centerline elevators moved airplanes from the flight to the hangar deck. Armament on the Essex class comprised 12 5"/38 guns in twin mounts, 32 40mm Bofors in dual and later in quad mounts (later increased to 72 in some carriers), and 46 20mm Swiss Oerlikon cannon (later increased to 60). The normal compliment of an Essex-class carrier was 91 aircraft, with a crew of more than 2,500 officers and sailors to support the carrier's air group. USS *Essex* was commissioned on December 31, 1942; by the end of the war the US Navy had commissioned 17 Essex-class carriers, though not all saw combat.

In contrast to the Essex-class carriers, the Independence class was a wartime expedient. President Franklin Roosevelt was the driving force behind the light carrier class. Concerned with the time it was expected to take for the *Essex* to be commissioned, Roosevelt pushed the Navy to convert some of the 10,000 ton Cleveland-class light cruisers the Navy had on order into aircraft carriers. After the attack on Pearl Harbor a previously reluctant Navy agreed, as now aircraft carriers had the highest priority. The Independence-class carriers had a shorter and narrower flight deck, 552ft by 73ft, a displacement that was one-third of the larger Essex class, an armament of 40mm and 20mm cannon, and a reduced aircraft complement of 24 fighters and nine torpedo bombers. While inferior to the Essex-class carriers in many respects, the great benefit of the Independence class was the speed of their construction. All nine conversions had been completed by the end of 1943, adding the equivalent of four Essex-class carriers to the Fast Carrier Task Force.

The Fast Carrier Task Force of 1944 was a far cry from the ad hoc carrier task forces of 1942. By mid-1944 the Fast Carrier Task Force comprised 15 or more Essex- and Independence-class carriers, up to eight fast battleships, a dozen cruisers, and as many as 75 destroyers. The Carrier Task Force was deployed in three to five independent task groups to ease maneuvering. Each task group functioned as an independent unit with its own carriers, usually two Essex class and two Independence class, and a defensive force of battleships, cruisers, and destroyers arrayed around the carriers to provide antiaircraft protection and defense against surface and submarine attacks. The task groups normally travelled 10–20 miles apart to facilitate concentration for air strikes and defense against enemy air attack. In September 1944, Task Force 38 contained the following Task Groups:

Task Group 38.1: *Hornet* (CV-12), *Wasp* (CV-18), *Belleau Wood* (CVL-24), *Cowpens* (CVL-25), *Monterey* (CVL-26)
Task Group 38.2: *Intrepid* (CV-11), *Bunker Hill* (CV-17), *Cabot* (CVL-28), *Independence* (CVL-22)
Task Group 38.3: *Essex* (CV-9), *Lexington* (CV-16), *Princeton* (CVL-23), *Langley* (CVL-27)
Task Group 38.4: *Franklin* (CV-13), *Enterprise* (CV-6), *San Jacinto* (CVL-30)

The carriers were the primary offensive weapon, and the role of the fast carriers was strategic, not tactical. The objective of the Fast Carrier Task Force was, like all naval forces before it, to obtain command of the sea. The fast carriers were intended to provide cover for the amphibious invasion fleets, neutralizing Japanese air power in areas near the planned invasion, and preventing the Japanese surface fleet from attacking the more vulnerable invasion force. The Fast Carrier Task Force was the vanguard of American air power, helping to capture advance bases for America's own land-based aircraft. In this regard, the Fast Carrier Task Force took on a new function, one not foreseen before the war: the destruction of the enemy's land-based air power.

A network of bases, pushed westward with the Navy's advance across the Pacific, supported the Carrier Task Force. The Pacific Fleet's main base was at Pearl Harbor, but the Navy set up large bases at Espiritu Santo in the New Hebrides, Eniwetok, at Manus in the Admiralty Islands, Guam and, in late September 1944, at Ulithi Atoll in the Caroline Islands. These

USS *Cowpens* (CVL-25) was an Independence-class carrier. These light carriers were a wartime expedient using cruiser hulls converted into aircraft carriers. Although their aircraft complement was less than the larger Essex-class carriers, the light carriers rapidly increased the number of carriers available to the US Navy. (NH 96206, NHHC)

16 ATTACKER'S CAPABILITIES

Battleships, cruisers, and destroyers formed the screen for the fast carriers, providing protection from air and sea attack. The North Carolina-class battleships, like USS *Washington* (BB-56) shown here, were floating antiaircraft batteries. Assigned to Task Group 38.3, the *Washington* carried 20 5"/38 caliber dual-purpose guns, 60 40mm Bofors cannon in 15 quadruple mounts, and 64 20mm cannon. (19-N-89065, NHHC)

bases provided maintenance and repair facilities and logistical support for the hundreds of ships in the Pacific Fleet. While at sea the 'fleet train', the fleet of tankers, transports, and escort carriers that provided all the fuel, supplies, and replacement aircraft the fast carriers needed, gave the Fast Carrier Task Force unprecedented mobility across the Pacific.

The core of the Fast Carrier Task Force's offensive power were the Carrier Air Groups (CAGs) and their trained air crews. Most of the air groups that participated in the September strikes on the Philippines had combat experience. Four air groups had been in action since January 1944 and three since May. In June 1944 the Navy changed the designation of its air groups to reflect the class of carrier they were assigned to. Air Groups assigned to Essex-class carriers were designated CVG, while those assigned to the Independence class became CVLG. In the summer of 1944 the standard complement of squadrons and aircraft remained the same as it had been for over a year. The larger CVG contained one fighter squadron with around 36 F6F Hellcats, one dive bomber squadron with 36 SB2C Helldivers, and one torpedo bomber squadron with 18 TBF or TBM Avengers. The smaller CVLG had one fighter squadron with 24 F6F Hellcats and one torpedo bomber squadron with nine TBM Avengers. There was, however, a change in thinking about the aircraft composition of air groups in the Essex-class fleet carriers.

In strikes against Japanese island bases and Japanese naval and merchant shipping, the Fast Carrier Task Force's dive bombers and torpedo bombers had been the principal offensive weapon. Now, as the prospect of attacking land-based air power in the Philippines, Formosa, and the Home islands came to the fore, the Hellcat (and later the F4U Corsair) would become the premier offensive weapon. For upcoming operations there would be a clear need for more fighters on the fleet carriers. One simple expedient was to replace dive bombers with Hellcats serving as fighter bombers. Several carrier fighter squadrons had used their Hellcats to bomb targets on Guam and Saipan during the invasion of the Marianas, and the Hellcat had proved successful as a fighter bomber. For the planned strikes against the Philippines, two squadrons were chosen to test this option, VB-2 from CVG-2 on board USS *Hornet*, and VB-14 from CVG-14 on board USS *Wasp*. VB-2 received 12 F6F-5 Hellcats to replace a like number of SB2C Helldivers, while VB-14 took on three F6F-3 and seven F6F-5 Hellcats, retaining 23 SB2C-3 Helldivers.

For the strikes on the Philippines, Task Force 38 had the following air groups:

Task Group 38.1: CVG-2 (*Hornet*), CVG-14 (*Wasp*), CVLG-21 (*Belleau Wood*), CVLG-22 (*Cowpens*), CVLG-28 (*Monterey*)
Task Group 38.2: CVG-18 (*Intrepid*), CVG-8 (*Bunker Hill*), CVLG-31 (*Cabot*), CVLGN-41 (*Independence*)
Task Group 38.3: CVG-15 (*Essex*), CVG-19 (*Lexington*), CVLG-27 (*Princeton*), CVLG-32 (*Langley*)
Task Group 38.4: CVG-13 (*Franklin*), CVG-20 (*Enterprise*), CVLG-51 (*San Jacinto*)

The fleet train of tankers and cargo ships allowed replenishment at sea, allowing the Fast Carrier Task Force to remain at sea for extended periods. Here USS *Hornet* (CV-12) and a cruiser refuel prior to strikes on the Bonin Islands in August 1944. (80G-367245, RG80, NARA)

Aircraft

The Grumman F6F Hellcat had been the premier US Navy carrier fighter for over a year. Powerful, ruggedly built, and heavily armed, the Hellcat broke the dominance of the Mitsubishi Zero-sen in the Pacific. Grumman had started building the F6F-5 in April 1944. After the invasion of the Marianas, the F6F-5 began replacing the F6F-3 in greater numbers. The F6F-5 featured several refinements, including a Pratt & Whitney R-2800-10W with water injection for greater power, a revised cowling and windshield, and aileron servo tabs which improved maneuverability. The Hellcat was proving to be a versatile aircraft and an effective fighter-bomber. The F6F-3 could carry a single 500lb or 1,000lb bomb on a bomb rack on the right inner wing.

The Erection and Maintenance Instructions for the F6F-5 state that the -5 model could carry 2,000lb of bombs. The bomb load could be either two 1,000lb bombs on racks on the inner wings, or one 2,000lb bomb on the centerline station underneath the bottom of the fuselage, or a single Mk 13 torpedo on the same station. The F6F-5 also had provision for carrying six 5" HAVR rockets under the wings. During the strikes over the Philippines, most F6F-3 and F6F-5 Hellcats carried a single 500lb bomb or 350lb depth charge with up to six 5" rockets.

Each CVG and CVLG had two to three F6F-3P or F6F-5P airplanes fitted with a long focal length camera on the lower left side of the fuselage just aft of the port wing. The photo reconnaissance Hellcats provided pre- and post-strike coverage of targets in the Philippines. The first night fighter version of the Hellcat, the F6F-3N with AN/APS-6 radar, provided coverage against intruders at night. As the Hellcat was easier to land on a carrier, the F6F-3N replaced the F4U-2 in the four-plane detachments serving on the large fleet carriers. Detachments of four F6F-3N night fighters from VFN-76, VFN-77, and VFN-78 served on *Bunker Hill*, *Enterprise*, *Essex*, *Franklin*, *Hornet*, *Intrepid*, *Lexington*, and *Wasp*. In addition to the separate detachments, USS *Independence* served as a dedicated night carrier with CVLGN-41. VFN-41, the night fighter component, had 14 F6F-3N night fighters, armed with the standard six .50 caliber Browning M-2 machine guns.

By August 1944, the Curtiss SB2C Helldiver had replaced the Douglas SBD-5 Dauntless in the dive bomber squadrons aboard the Essex-class carriers. The Helldiver had a difficult gestation and required many modifications to make it suitable for combat and operations from a carrier. It remained a demanding aircraft to fly compared to the more forgiving SBD Dauntless. The SB2C-1 made its combat debut in November 1943, followed by the SB2C-1C with two 20mm cannon replacing the four .50 caliber machine guns in the wings. Prior to the strikes on the Philippines, four out of the six dive bomber squadrons on the

ATTACKER'S CAPABILITIES

Over the summer of 1944 the F6F-5 began to replace the F6F-3 in the carrier air group fighter squadrons (VF). The F6F-5 featured several improvements over the F6F-3, including the ability to carry a heavier bomb load and HVAR rockets under the wings. (80G-228882, RG80, NARA)

Essex-class carriers replaced their SB2C-1Cs with the newer SB2C-3 which had a more powerful Wright R-2600-20 engine offering 1,900hp, giving a small increase in maximum speed at the cost of slightly less range. The dive-bomber squadrons considered the SB2C-3 to be a vast improvement over the SB2C-1, the additional power particularly important for take-offs from the carriers. The SB2C-1C and SB2C-3 could carry 2,000lb of bombs, 1,000lb internally in the bomb bay and 1,000lb under the wings. In strikes on Chichi Jima on August 31, 1944, VB-20's SB2C-3Cs used a Douglas DPG-1 gun package containing two .50 caliber machine guns carrying 285 rounds per gun as a normal load. These were attached to the Helldiver's underwing bomb racks, giving the SB2C the firepower of four .50 calibers and two 20 mm cannon for strafing.

The Grumman TBF/General Motors TBM Avenger served in the torpedo bomber squadrons on both Essex- and Independence-class carriers. The General Motors-built TBM-1C was steadily replacing the Grumman TBF-1C in the air groups. The portly Avenger

An SB2C-3 belonging to VB-19 taxis forward and folds its wings after landing aboard USS *Lexington* (CV-16) in August 1944. By this point in the war the SB2C had replaced the SBD Dauntless in the dive-bomber squadrons (VB) on the Essex-class carriers. The SB2C-3 had a more powerful Wright R-2600 engine which improved its flying qualities. (80G-268126, RG80, NARA)

was a large airplane, with a wingspan that was three-quarters the width of the flight deck on an Independence-class carrier. What it lacked in maneuverability was compensated for by its steadiness when launching a torpedo and its ease of deck landing. The internal bomb bay could carry, alternatively, one Mk 13 torpedo, one 2,000lb bomb, one 1,000lb bomb, four 500lb bombs, or 12 100lb bombs. The Avenger had a nominal combat radius of 260 miles with a full combat load, but this could be extended with two 58-gallon underwing drop tanks. The TBM-1C also had underwing attachments for up to eight 5" HAVR rockets. The TBM-1D carried an ASD-1 (AN/APS-3) centimetric search radar in a radome on the starboard edge of the wing which gave a search radius of 40 miles. Two TBM-1Ds served with VT-14 and VT-15 during the Philippine strikes while VTN-41 carried eight TBM-1Ds on the *Independence*.

Targets and tactics

The objective of the September carrier strikes on the Philippines was to inflict the maximum possible damage to Japanese military forces. The primary targets were shipping, port installations, aircraft, and air bases. The three Navy carrier airplanes in Task Force 38 – the F6F Hellcat, SB2C Helldiver, and TBF/TBM Avenger – all played a role in attacking these targets.

After two and a half years of war, the US Navy had decided on the most effective formations and tactics for its fighter, dive bomber, and torpedo bomber squadrons. As the Navy's tactical orders and doctrine for carrier aircraft stated: "The war has taught many lessons which have been learned the hard way – *by losses.*" The tactics the carrier air groups employed in September 1944 had been proven in combat. The basic tactical unit for all squadrons was the division, consisting of two sections of two aircraft in fighter squadrons, and two sections of three aircraft in dive and torpedo bomber squadrons. Two or more divisions could be combined into larger formations for increased striking power. The Navy had developed formations that were flexible, simple to fly, maneuverable, and that could respond to rapid developments in offensive or defensive conditions. The horizontal and vertical space between aircraft within a section or a division, or group of divisions, depended on the type of aircraft and the nature of the mission. Squadrons practiced flying formations of one or multiple divisions, with aircraft or divisions stepped up or stepped down, learning to maintain formations through constant practice.

The Japanese Army and Navy forces in the Philippines were dependent on shipments of ammunition, equipment, fuel, provisions and clothing, weapons, and parts from other areas of the Empire, particularly from the Home Islands. The Army and the Navy had their own separate supply channels and allocated merchant shipping which created unnecessary duplication of effort. Japanese shipping losses compounded the problems of supplying forces in the southern

Navy pilots began training in aerial gunnery during their intermediate training and would undertake more intensive work in gunnery and gunnery approaches in operational training. Practice was relentless until approaches became second nature. (80G-475244, RG80, NARA)

OPPOSITE STRAFING TACTICS FOR FIGHTERS

When escorting fighters encountered no enemy air opposition on shipping strikes, the fighters would drop down to strafe before and after the dive and torpedo bombers made their attacks. The fighters would shift to an echelon formation before beginning their strafing runs and approach the target from different angles to distract the antiaircraft gunners on the ship. The leader would pull out at 1,500ft, with each other plane pulling out slightly lower, and retiring at low altitude until out of range.

region. By August 1944, Allied aircraft and submarines had sunk more than half of the Japanese merchant shipping fleet. Large capacity freighters of over 1,000 gross weight tons were not the only shipping targets. With the exception of the railroad system on Luzon, merchant shipping was the only means of supplying Japanese troops and air units on the Philippine Islands. Smaller vessels, in the 250–1,000 gross weight ton range, were critical to transferring supplies from main ports to the outer islands. Damaging a merchant vessel could be almost as disruptive as sinking a ship. A damaged vessel had to remain in harbor for repair for some period of time, disrupting shipping schedules, and placing a burden on undamaged vessels as well as port facilities. Bombing port facilities had similar repercussions. Ships could not unload cargo at damaged ports or undergo repairs, while destroying warehouses in port areas also destroyed the materials stored inside. Damage to shipping and ports had a ripple effect down the supply chain to ground and air units and naval vessels. A lack of fuel meant fewer flying hours for pilot trainees while a lack of a part could ground an aircraft leaving it open to destruction in an attack on an airfield.

Dive bombing was considered an aircraft carrier's primary offensive weapon against shipping and fixed targets. In tests before the war, dive bombing had proved to be three to four times more effective than horizontal bombing. Dive bombers were also thought to be less susceptible to attack from enemy fighters than torpedo bombers. The US Navy's tactical doctrine for dive bombing squadrons stressed "the rapid and accurate delivery of heavy bombs" as the ultimate objective of dive bombing. Accurate delivery of the bombs depended on weather conditions, the nature of the target, enemy aerial opposition, and antiaircraft defenses.

The basic tactical formation was the division. Fighter squadron divisions comprised two sections of two aircraft, while dive bomber and torpedo squadrons flew in divisions of two sections of three aircraft. If enemy aircraft were expected over the target, the bombers would approach in a tight defensive formation. (80G-238780, RG80, NARA)

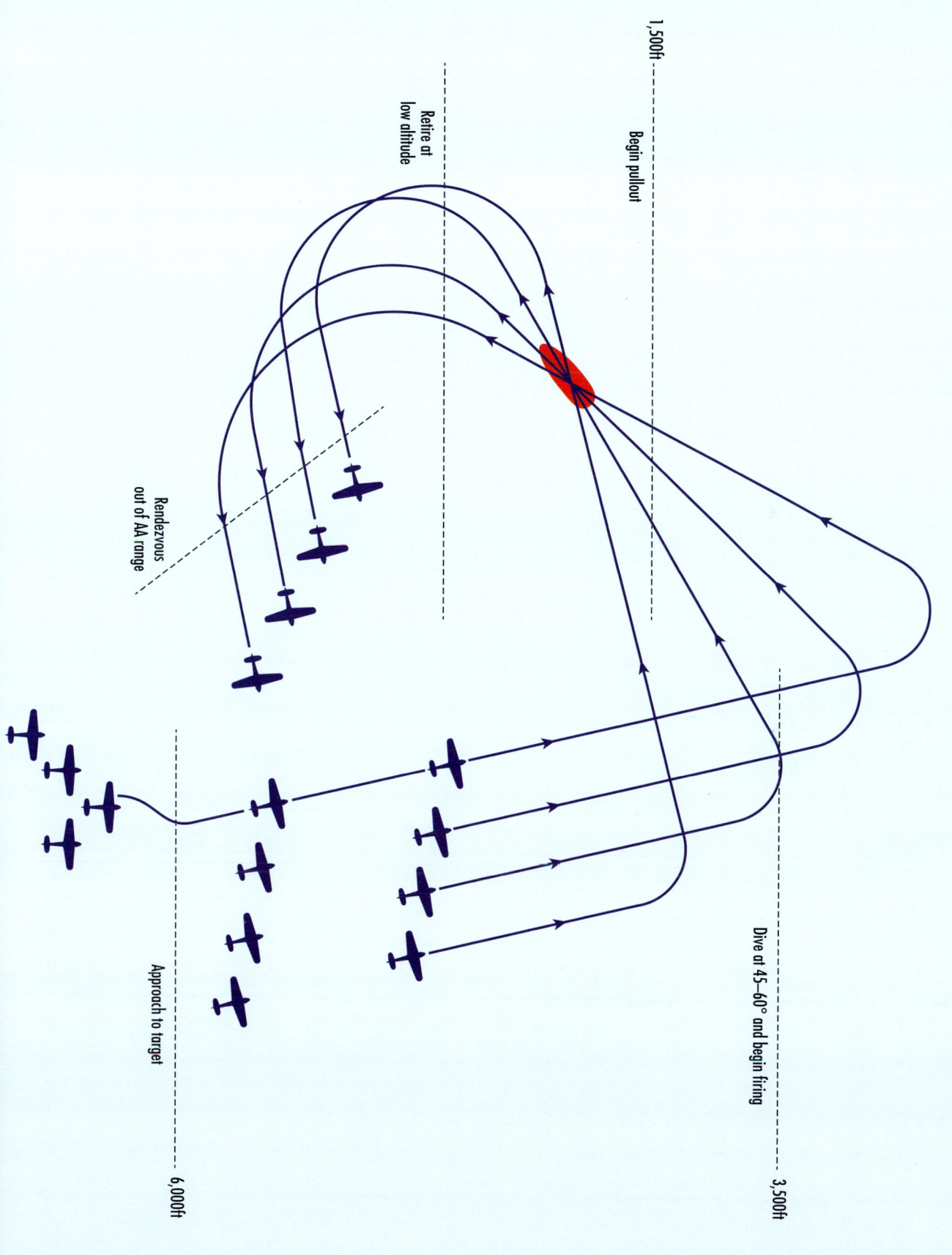

Multiple divisions of dive bombers could be used in an attack. The sequence of attack was first, the approach; second, the dive; and third, the rendezvous after the attack. The approach to the target required dive bomber squadrons to fly at 20,000ft if weather permitted. During the approach, divisions were to remain closed-up for mutual defense against fighter attack. Ideally, once having sighted the target, the attack formation would approach in a straight line toward the target, gradually losing altitude before entering the final dive between 12,000ft and 15,000ft. Each airplane in the division would make an individual attack.

Before entering the final dive on a moving target, the pilot would determine his point of aim and place his sight ahead of the target so that his sight would drift to the desired release point during his dive. Diving to the minimum altitude release point consistent with the blast effect of the bombs carried and restrictions on pull out for the airplane greatly increased bombing accuracy. While bombing by sections was sometimes used, experience had shown that single-plane dives, spaced a few seconds apart, resulted in a greater number of hits on the target and presented enemy antiaircraft gunners with multiple targets. After pulling out of the dive, pilots were to leave the target area at high speed and following different courses to avoid antiaircraft fire. Selection of a rendezvous point depended on the direction of the attack, enemy antiaircraft dispositions, and possible aerial opposition. Pilots were instructed to immediately close-up with other friendly planes to ensure mutual support.

Dive bomber squadrons employed glide bombing and low-level bombing when the ceiling and visibility precluded diving from higher altitudes. The angle of the dive in glide bombing was between 45 to 55 degrees, without dive brakes, releasing bombs at around 1,500ft. A glide bombing or low-level bombing attack was often preceded by fighters strafing the target just before the bombers made their approach. During the September carrier strikes, a typical bomb load for an SB2C attacking shipping was a single 1,000lb semi-armor piercing (SAP) bomb, which provided greater penetration than the standard general purpose (GP) bomb, with two 250lb GP bombs also carried.

The primary mission of carrier torpedo bomber squadrons was to sink enemy naval and merchant shipping with their torpedoes. Like dive bomber squadrons, torpedo squadrons were organized into divisions of six aircraft in two sections. A successful torpedo attack depended on the skill of individual pilots who had to estimate the speed, angle, and distance of the target, but who also had to be prepared to meet unexpected changes in the tactical situation. The general principles of torpedo attack were first and foremost an accurate determination of the dropping range to the target. Torpedoes had a fixed run of underwater travel before they

The Fast Carrier Task Force employed dive bombers for effective attacks against shipping and targets on land using dive bombing and glide bombing. The SB2Cs normally carried a bombload of one 1,000lb bomb in the bomb bay and two 250lb bombs under the wings. (NHHC S.475.0P1, NHHC)

became armed, and as airspeeds increased, the dropping range lengthened. The range had to be adequate for the torpedo to become armed, but short enough so that the target vessel couldn't maneuver away from the attack. In an attack, a division of torpedo planes would approach a target from ahead and spread out from 90 to 135 degrees, approaching from different angles. The ideal attack was called 'the anvil', where the target's evasive maneuvers would expose the vessel to a hit from some of the torpedoes. Torpedo doctrine called for a minimum of six airplanes for an attack on a capital ship, closely coordinated with a preceding dive bombing attack.

The objective of an attack on an enemy airfield was to neutralize enemy air power. This was often difficult to achieve. Much depended on the nature of the mission, whether the objective was the temporary or sustained neutralization of the airfield. Temporary neutralization for a few hours or a few days could be achieved through destroying aircraft on the ground and damaging the landing areas on the field, while sustained neutralization required bombing airfield installations that supported aircraft including hangars, repair facilities, storage facilities, fuel and ammunition dumps, and ancillary buildings. The most efficient means of damaging or destroying aircraft on the ground was through strafing, though the new 5" HAVR rockets offered an alternative that was less dangerous given its longer range. Landing areas – runways and taxiways – could be damaged with high explosive bombs to create craters, although this damage would be temporary as craters could be easily filled and repaired. Fragments from bombs dropped on runways could also damage nearby aircraft on the ground. Experience had shown that a 100lb GP bomb was most effective for cratering landing areas.

Bombing airfield installations could cause more long-lasting and disruptive damage. Hangars were not necessary for storing aircraft in the tropics, but they provided an area for maintenance, repair, and assembly of aircraft. The objective was not the destruction of the hangar but the contents within. Hangars contained tools, repair and assembly equipment, and spare parts that if lost would delay maintenance and repair of damaged aircraft. This required a GP bomb of 500lb or greater. Similarly, destroying repair and storage facilities,

VB-14 exchanged ten of its SB2C-3 Helldivers for ten F6F-3/5 Hellcats as an experiment in replacing the dive bombers with fighter bombers. Here Lt (jg) C.J Haggerty climbs aboard one of the squadron's F6F-3 Hellcats prior to a mission. Haggerty claimed a Ki-27 Nate damaged on September 9 and a Ki-61 Tony damaged on September 21, demonstrating the versatility of the Hellcat as a fighter and fighter bomber. (80G-258440, RG80, NARA)

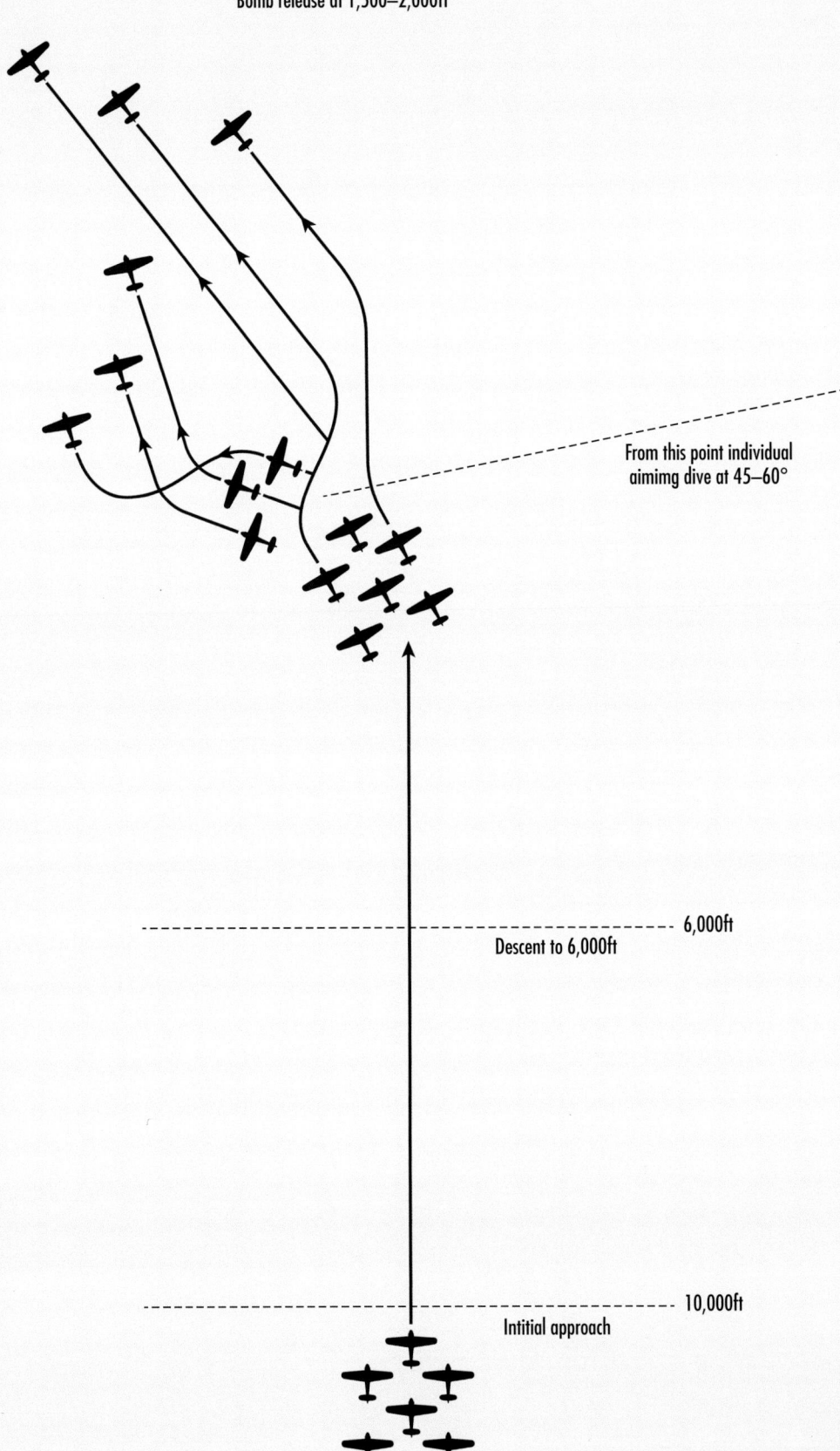

OPPOSITE GLIDE BOMBING ATTACK DOCTRINE

Glide bombing proved to be an effective bombing technique that could be used by different carrier aircraft. In the majority of sorties flown by the torpedo squadrons, the TBM Avengers carried bombs instead of torpedoes. The usual bomb load was three or four 500lb bombs, or ten 100lb bombs. Divisions maintained a fighter defense formation as they approached a target. Descending to 8,000–10,000ft, each of the two sections would break away from the target to allow airplanes to spread out before each pilot began an individual aiming dive at an angle of 45–60 degrees, beginning at 4,000–6,000ft, with bomb release at 1,500–2,000ft. Recovery entailed remaining at high speed and low altitude until out of the range of antiaircraft fire.

particularly facilities storing fuel, ammunition, and spare parts could severely restrict operations from an airfield.

The dive bomber squadrons used tactics that were similar to strikes against shipping, approaching the target area by divisions at medium altitude then entering individual dives on specific targets. On certain missions the dive bombers would target concentrations of heavy antiaircraft guns ahead of the following strike forces. On strikes against airfields in the Philippines the SB2Cs normally carried one 1,000lb GP bomb and two 100lb or 250lb bombs under the wings. As they descended, the dive bombers would often strafe the target area with their 20mm wing cannon. After pulling out of their dives the rear gunners would open fire with their twin .30 caliber machine guns.

Glide bombing attacks by torpedo bombers followed the same basic principles that dive bombers employed, using a dive angle of 45 to 60 degrees, beginning the attack from an altitude of 8,000–10,000ft, and releasing the bombs at 1,500–2,000ft above the target. Once sighting the target, a squadron would split into divisions for the attack. Each division would break from its tight fighter defense formation, with each section breaking away from the target then turning back in to allow individual airplanes to take different approaches to the target; pilots were admonished not to follow the preceding airplane in the dive. The final aiming dive would have the airplane lined up with the target with little correction needed in the dive. In the approach and initial dive, much depended on the strength and pattern of antiaircraft fire. The torpedo bombers normally carried two to four 500lb GP bombs on these strikes, but sometimes the heavier 2,000lb GP bomb.

The role of fighter aircraft was always, first and foremost, to protect the strike force aircraft and the task force from enemy aircraft. The secondary mission for fighters was offensive, to attack enemy air and surface forces and installations, flying fighter sweeps ahead of the strike force to clear the target area of enemy fighters and strafe antiaircraft positions. There were four basic principles of fighter combat:

Superiority of Position: Fighters must maintain superior altitude to enemy aircraft and stay between enemy aircraft and their objectives.
Superiority of Disposition: Fighter formations should have the most efficient employment of their numbers.
Superiority of Concentration: Divisions and sections should always be in a position to provide mutual support.
Superiority of Marksmanship: The ability to hit a target with the first burst, to make effective runs against a target, careful selection of the point of aim, and conservation of ammunition.

Offensively, Navy fighter doctrine stressed bracketing a target, placing sections or divisions abeam of a target to the left and right so that if the enemy aircraft turned in any direction it would move into a favorable firing position for either section or division. In bracketing a target, a section or division could easily shift in to the beam defense formation (what was

Navy doctrine was to send a fighter sweep to the target area just before the first strike arrived. The fighters would clear the air of any enemy aircraft before the dive and torpedo bombers began their bomb runs. This photo, taken later in the year, captures an F6F Hellcat setting fire to a Zero-sen over the Philippines. (80G-46984, RG80, NARA)

earlier called the Thach Weave after Lt Cdr John Thach, who developed the maneuver). If a section or division flying abeam of one another was attacked from front or rear, one of the aircraft or sections would turn into the other, bringing the attacking enemy aircraft into the line of fire of one of the aircraft, sections, or divisions. Weaving continuously provided mutual protection against attack. The beam defense formation could also be employed when escorting the strike force. Divisions assigned to close cover or high cover could weave above the strike formation to defend against attacks from any direction.

Air crew

Task Force 38 held a decided advantage over the Japanese Army and Navy air units in the Philippines in the quality and experience of the Task Force's air crews. The Task Force had many more capable pilots on strength with hundreds of hours of flying time and, in many cases, combat experience in the months prior to the strikes on the Philippines. Many of the fighter, dive bomber, and torpedo bomber squadron commanders were graduates of the US Naval Academy who had become naval aviators before the war and had served on carriers and often as flying instructors before taking up their current commands. The core of the carrier squadrons were the young junior officers, the lieutenants and lieutenants junior grade who led divisions or sections within a division. These younger men had typically joined the Navy after the attack on Pearl Harbor through one of the Navy's recruiting programs for

A photo of pilots of VF-14 taken on board USS *Wasp* (CV-18) at the end of August 1944. The training these pilots had received was superior to that of the average Imperial Japanese Navy or Army pilot they encountered over the Philippines. (80G-349718, RG80, NARA)

Naval Reserve officers, completing their flying training during 1942 and 1943. In the fighter squadrons, many of the pilots who claimed Japanese aircraft during the September strikes had already made claims in previous air battles, particularly during the Marianas Turkey Shoot in June 1944.

The new ensigns joining the carrier squadrons during the summer of 1944 had gone through the Navy's wartime training program which emphasized specialization at an earlier stage of training than in the Navy's prewar training program. After 16 weeks of primary training, the aviation cadet would advance to 20 weeks of intermediate training. In the third phase of intermediate training the cadet would be directed to a specific type of airplane such as carrier airplanes, patrol bombers, or observation aircraft, and his training organized accordingly. Pilots destined for carrier aircraft would train on the North American SNJ and begin learning combat tactics. The key wartime innovation in Navy aviation training was dedicated operational training, formally conducted at the squadron level, where a newly minted ensign would be introduced to the airplane he would fly in combat. In the eight to 12 week program of operational training, the new pilot would qualify in an operational airplane, fly practice combat missions under the guidance of an experienced pilot recently returned from combat, and become qualified to land on a carrier. By the time a replacement pilot reached the fleet, he would have acquired several hundred hours of flying time. In August–September, the replacement pilots joining VB-14 in CVG-14 had an average of just over 500 hours flying time, including hours on the SB2C Helldiver. As will be seen, this was a great contrast to Japanese pilots in the Philippines.

DEFENDER'S CAPABILITIES
The Japanese in the Philippines

Air units and commanders

The Japanese Navy had few capable reconnaissance aircraft available in the Philippines, having to rely on a small number of Nakajima J1N1-C Type 2 Reconnaissance Aircraft ("Irving"). (2008-03-31_Image_610_01, Peter M. Bowers Collection, Museum of Flight, Seattle, WA)

Following their defeats and severe losses in the air battles over New Guinea and the Marianas, the Japanese Army and Navy air commands retreated to the Philippines to begin rebuilding their strength for the *Sho* operations. At the beginning of 1944, the Imperial Army's 4th Air Army (4th Kōkūgun) commanded the 6th and 7th Air Divisions (6th and 7th Hikōshidan) covering New Guinea and the eastern regions of the Dutch East Indies. The 6th Air Division suffered severe losses in the battle for Hollandia, and the 7th Air Division was ordered to advance to New Guinea to support the battered 6th Air Division, but also sustained heavy losses over Biak and withdrew back to the Dutch East Indies. In early June, the 4th Air Army transferred its headquarters from Menado in the Celebes to Manila on Luzon, to take command of all Army air units in the Philippines and to build the 6th and 7th Air Divisions back to strength, with the 7th Air Division remaining in the Dutch East Indies. To build up air defenses in the Philippines, the Imperial Army transferred the 2nd and 4th Air Divisions from the 2nd Field Army in Manchuria to the Philippines.

In June, the Imperial Army transferred the 17th and 19th Air Regiments (17th and 19th Sentai), equipped with the Kawasaki Ki-61 Type 3 Fighter Hien ("Tony"), to the Philippines to form the 22nd Air Brigade (22nd Hikōdan). In July the 30th and 31st Air Regiments, flying the Nakajima Ki-43 II Type 1 fighter Hayabusa ("Oscar") left their bases in Manchuria for the Philippines where they formed the 13th Air Brigade (13th Hikōdan). Both the 13th and 22nd Air Brigades came under the command of the 2nd Air Division. By the end of July 1944 the 2nd Air Division had added three more air brigades, the 6th, 7th, and 10th to its strength in the Philippines. The 6th Air Brigade comprised the 65th and 66th Assault Regiments with the Mitsubishi Ki-51 Type 99 Assault Aircraft ("Sonia"). The 7th Air Brigade had two heavy bomber regiments, the 12th Air Regiment still flying the Mitsubishi Ki-21 Type 97 Heavy Bomber ("Sally") and the 62nd Air Regiment with the newer Nakajima Ki-49-II Type 100 Heavy Bomber ("Helen"). The 10th Air Brigade was a fighter bomber brigade with the 45th Air Regiment which had converted from the Kawasaki

Ki-48 Type 99 Twin-engine Light Bomber to the Kawasaki Ki-45 Type 2 Twin-engine Fighter ("Nick"). For reconnaissance, the 2nd Air Division had the 2nd Sentai and one squadron of the 28th Sentai equipped with the Mitsubishi Ki-46 Type 100 Command Reconnaissance Aircraft ("Dinah"). By the end of August 1944 the 2nd Air Division had approximately 420 airplanes in the Philippines with a little over 300 airplanes operational. The 2nd Air Division's units were deployed at Clark Field on Luzon and at Bacolod airfield on the island of Negros in the central Philippines. In addition to these first line units, the Japanese Army Air Force had established at least nine Flying Training Units in the Philippines with several hundred training aircraft, including around 60 Nakajima Ki-27 Type 97 Fighter Aircraft ("Nate") serving as advanced trainers. The 4th Air Division, assigned to the Philippines at the same time as the 2nd Air Division, consisted mostly of maintenance personnel assigned to bases around the Philippines.

In August 1944, Lt Gen Tominaga Kyoji arrived in Manila to take command of the 4th Air Army. Tominaga was an odd choice for command. Not only did he have no experience with Army aviation, but he had also spent nearly his entire career in staff positions, most recently as Vice Minister of War under General Tojo Hideki. Apparently even Emperor Hirohito questioned his appointment given his lack of knowledge of aviation. While the officers commanding the air brigades and the air regiments did have experience – for example, Col Monnosuke Ono who had commanded the 6th Air Brigade since December 1943 and Maj Nishi Susumu, CO of the 31st Air Regiment who had been flying with the regiment since 1942 – disease and long service in the tropics had debilitated many 4th Air Army senior officers.

The Imperial Navy faced the same task of building up the strength of its air units in the Philippines in preparation for the *Sho* operation. Following its nearly complete annihilation during the battle for the Philippines, Admiral Toyoda Soemu, who had taken over command of the Combined Fleet in May 1944, assigned the remnants of the First Air Fleet to the Philippines where it was to be reorganized and rebuilt. During July, the Navy transferred the flying elements of the 23rd Air Flotilla (23rd Kōkū Sentai) in the Celebes and the 26th and 61st Air Flotillas (26th and 61st Kōkū Sentai) at Davao to the First Air Fleet, then reorganizing in Japan. The 153rd Naval Air Group (153rd Kōkūtai), a mixed fighter and reconnaissance unit in the 23rd Air Flotilla now assigned to the First Air Fleet, gave up its squadron of Zero-sen ("Zeke") fighters (Sento 311 Hikōtai) in exchange for a night fighter squadron (Sento 901 Hikōtai) with 24 Nakajima J1N1-S Gekko ("Irving") and A6M5 Zero-sen night fighters.

The 201st Naval Air Group (201st Kōkūtai) came from the 26th Air Flotilla, having suffered heavy losses against US Navy carrier fighters at Truk and Saipan, and having

Although he had no experience with aviation, Lt Gen Tominaga Kyoji was appointed commander of the Japanese Army Air Force's Fourth Air Army in September 1944. (Wikimedia/Public Domain)

OPPOSITE LOCATION OF JAPANESE AIRFIELDS IN THE PHILIPPINES

transferred to Davao to be reconstituted, taking in remaining pilots from other fighter units disbanded after the Marianas debacle. By September 1, the 201st had four squadrons of A6M5 Zero-sen fighters (Sento 301, 305, 306, and 311 Hikōtai) with 210 aircraft, of which 130 were operational. The 61st Air Flotilla provided the 761st Naval Air Group (761st Kōkūtai), a bomber unit with the Mitsubishi G4M Type 1 Attack Bomber ("Betty") and the Yokosuka P1Y1 Navy Bomber Ginga ("Frances"), and the 1021st Naval Air Group (1021st Kōkūtai), a transport unit operating several types of transport aircraft. By the beginning of September, the First Air Fleet had a strength of just over 400 aircraft, of which 249 were serviceable. Most Navy air units were based at Cebu or on Mindanao.

In August, a new First Air Fleet established its headquarters at Davao on Mindanao, moving to the Clark airfield complex north of Manila a month later. Vice Admiral Teraoka Kinpei was appointed commander of the 1st Air Fleet arriving at Davao on August 12. In contrast to his Army counterpart, Teraoka was no stranger to aviation, having commanded aircraft carriers before the war and the 11th Combined Air Group from February to August 1944, just before his transfer to the Philippines. He now had the unenviable task of building up his air units and his air bases as rapidly as possible.

In contrast, Vice Admiral Teraoka Kinpei had extensive experience in naval aviation when he was appointed commander of the 1st Air Fleet on August 7, 1944. Despite his best efforts to build up an effective force for the defense of the Philippines, he would last only 74 days in command. (Wikimedia/Public Domain)

An unidentified Japanese airfield on Negros showing the general arrangement of the airfields the Japanese built or enlarged in the Philippines. The photo was taken on September 14, 1944. Note the extensive taxiways and revetments away from the airstrip to limit damage from air attacks. (Carrier Air Group Action Report for September 1944, RG 38, NARA)

Bases and facilities

After the Japanese Army completed its conquest of the Philippines in April 1942, the area became something of a back water, a third-level base area far removed from the fighting in the Central and South Pacific. The Army established a garrison force and began building or improving airfields in the Philippines stretching from Luzon to Mindanao, completing 13 airfields. Manila became a focal point for air routes from Japan to the Japanese-occupied territories in Southeast Asia and the South Pacific. As the Japanese Army expanded its pilot training programs it established advanced flying training units in the Philippines as well as in other countries in Southeast Asia. The Imperial Navy, too, utilized airfields in the Philippines for pilot training and established seaplane bases in several locations. In March 1944 the Navy established the 31st Naval Air Group (31st Kōkūtai) at Manila and the 32nd Naval Air Group (32nd Kōkūtai) at Sarangani in Mindanao to train enlisted pilots who formed the bulk of the Imperial Navy's air crews.

Japan's Imperial General Headquarters (IGHQ) instructed the Japanese Fourteenth Army, defending the Philippines, to make improvements to existing air bases and add an additional 30 airfields, the plans to be completed by March 1944. The 4th Air Division took on responsibility for airfield construction, using troops from the Fourteenth Army. In early 1944 the Navy decided to convert some of its advanced training bases to operational airfields and to develop new airfield sites around Davao and Manila, intending to add 21 new airfields by the end of 1944.

By the beginning of September 1944 the island of Luzon held the largest number of airfields. There were ten airfields built around the prewar Clark Field. Clark Field No. 1 (or Clark Center) could hold more than 300 airplanes, while Clark North could hold from 200 to 300 aircraft. Mabalacat East and West, to the north of the Clark Field complex, had a capacity of up to 200 airplanes, while the four satellite airfields to the south (Angeles North, South, East, and West) could hold an additional 300 aircraft. There were multiple runways, revetments, hangars, and other buildings. There were five airfields around Manila, with the old Nichols Field, the largest in the Manila area, having been built up to hold 200 to 300 aircraft and Nielson Field, another prewar airfield, holding up to 200 more. Seven other smaller nearby fields held 50 to 100 aircraft.

In the Visayas in the central Philippines, the airfields were concentrated on the east coast of Leyte and on the north coast of Negros. Tacloban, and San Pedro on Leyte could hold from 50 to 100 airplanes. The northwest coast of Negros had four airfields, with Bacolod being the largest with a capacity of up to 200 airplanes and nearby satellite fields holding up to 50 aircraft. On the north coast of Negros there were three smaller fields, including Fabrica, while a further three small airfields were located on the central east coast of Cebu, which could hold from 50 to 100 aircraft. The Navy had built six airfields around Davao on Mindanao, with a smaller group of airfields around the prewar airfield at Del Monte. The wide span of airfields across the Philippines, north and south, east and west, theoretically

The Japanese greatly expanded the prewar Clark Field, adding more runways and extensive taxiways and revetments, and more airfields in the area around Clark Field. The Clark Field complex became a key target for Fifth Air Force B-24 bombers and for Task Force 38. (3A-31199, RG342FH, NARA)

gave Japanese units the ability to stage attacks on an enemy invasion force from multiple directions, swiftly reinforcing one area from another.

While the number of air bases built up by September 1944 was impressive, in reality there were many shortcomings. In a postwar analysis, the Imperial Navy considered that of all its preparations for air combat in the Philippines, its preparation of its bases was the poorest. There were delays in concluding negotiations with the Army, changes in plans for using particular bases, the hurried reorganization of the newly assigned air units, and difficulties in transporting supplies and equipment. In particular, preparations for rear area bases were incomplete by the time Task Force 38 attacked.

The Japanese in the Philippines did however recognize the importance of radar, and had started to increase the number of radar stations. The Navy was ahead of the Army in radar development and established air search radars in several locations in the Philippine Islands, using fixed, mobile, and portable radar units. The communications net connecting the radar stations to command headquarters in key target areas was inadequate. The time spent transmitting information was excessive. On several occasions, warnings of approaching carrier aircraft arrived too late.

Aircraft and weapons

The Japanese Army and Navy shared responsibility for the defense of the Philippines, though with no overall unifying command structure there was little coordination between the two services. The types of aircraft the Army and Navy deployed in the Philippines had all been in service for several years. There were few of the newest aircraft types available, particularly with regard to fighter aircraft. The new Kawanishi N1K1-J Shiden Navy fighter ("George") and the Nakajima Ki-84 Type 4 Fighter Hayate ("Frank") arrived in the Philippines after the September carrier strikes as part of the *Sho-1* operation forces.

Japanese Navy mechanics refuel a Zero-sen from a hand cart. Although outclassed by the latest American fighters, the A6M5 Model 52 Zero-Sen remained the Imperial Navy's principal fighter aircraft as production of the new Kawanishi N1K1-J Shiden ("George") was still building up. (80G-169292, RG80, NARA)

The Imperial Navy's fighter units relied on the Mitsubishi A6M Zero-sen ("Zeke"), still the Navy's predominant fighter, although now outclassed by the American F6F Hellcat and F4U Corsair. The A6M5 was now the predominant version of the Zero, featuring improved performance and armament. Two belt-fed Type 99 Model 2 Mk 4 20mm cannon in the wings replaced the earlier drum-fed model, providing 125 rounds per gun (rpg), an increase of 25rpg. The A6M5b replaced one of the nose-mounted 7.7mm machine guns with a more powerful 13.2mm machine gun. In capable hands the Zero-sen could still be a dangerous opponent, particularly if a Hellcat pilot made the mistake of trying to maneuver with a Zero at lower airspeeds.

The Navy employed several types of bombers in the Philippines. The 761st Kōkūtai continued to use the Mitsubishi G4M Attack Bomber ("Betty") though it stood little chance against the Hellcat. The new Yokosuka P1Y1 Navy Bomber Ginga ("Frances") was nearly a hundred miles an hour faster than the G4M, though it lacked the Betty's long range. The P1Y1 had one flexible Type 99 20mm cannon in the nose and one rear-firing Type 99 20mm cannon or a Type 2 13.2mm machine gun for protection. The Ginga could carry one 1,764lb torpedo or up to 2,205lb of bombs internally. Lacking sufficient reconnaissance aircraft, the Navy used the P1Y1 on searches for the American Task Groups off the Philippines.

DEFENDER'S CAPABILITIES

The Nakajima Ki-43-II Type 1 fighter was still the Japanese Army's principal fighter, but like the Zero-Sen, outclassed by fighters like the F6F Hellcat. Its only advantage in combat with the Hellcat was its superior maneuverability. (2008-3-31_Image_608_01, Peter M. Bowers Collection, Museum of Flight)

The Aichi D3A Type 99 Carrier Bomber ("Val") was still in service in the Philippines, though by now considered obsolete. The 201st Kōkūtai apparently had several Yokosuka D4Y2 Navy Carrier Dive Bombers ("Judy"), the fastest dive bomber in service with any navy, assigned to the unit. The Navy had to rely on the small number of Nakajima J1N1-C Type 2 Reconnaissance Aircraft Gekko ("Irving") in the 153rd Kōkūtai for reconnaissance as well. The J1N1-C had a maximum speed of 329mph and a range of nearly 1,700 miles.

The Japanese Army's 30th and 31st Air Regiments were both equipped with the Nakajima Ki 43-II Hayabusa ("Oscar") armed with two 12.7mm machine guns in the nose. With a top speed of 330mph the Hayabusa was exceptionally maneuverable, and could out-maneuver a Hellcat with ease. On one occasion over Negros, the attacking Hellcat pilots were astonished to see an Oscar carry out a split-S maneuver from 1,200ft altitude and pull out safely. With no armor protection and unprotected fuel tanks, an Oscar had little chance of surviving a blast from a Hellcat's six .50 caliber machine guns. Although it is uncertain which unit they were assigned to, Hellcat pilots reported numerous combats with the Nakajima Ki 44-IIb Type 2 Single-engine Fighter Shoki ("Tojo") during the strikes on the Visayas. The Tojo was designed as an interceptor, with a heavier armament than the Oscar of four 12.7mm machine guns, two in the nose and two in the wings. Several of the Army's advanced training units flew the older Nakajima Ki 27 Fighter ("Nate"), which stood no chance against a Hellcat.

During the September carrier strikes, Task Force 38's Hellcat squadrons encountered the Kawasaki Ki 61 Type 3 Fighter Hien ("Tony") for the first time. Powered by a 1,100hp liquid-cooled engine, the Ki 61-I KAI had a maximum speed of 366mph and a comparatively heavy armament of two Ho-5 20mm cannon and two Ho-103 12.7mm machine guns. Hellcat

The most capable Japanese Army fighter airplane in the Philippines in September 1944 was the Kawasaki Ki-61 Type 3 fighter, which equipped the 17th and 19th Fighter Regiments. This photo shows a derelict Ki-61 belonging to the 19th Fighter Regiment captured on Luzon. (3A-30387, RG342FH, NARA)

The Kawasaki Ki-45 Type 2 two-seat fighter equipped the 45th Fighter Regiment, formerly a light bomber regiment. Some of the Regiment's Type 2 fighters were equipped with two 20mm cannon mounted obliquely behind the cockpit. Though a capable interceptor, the Ki-45 had difficulty combating the Hellcat. (3A-30389, RG342FH, NARA)

pilots found the Tony a tougher nut to crack. The Tony could out-turn and out-climb the Hellcat at certain speeds (though the Hellcat could easily catch a Tony in a dive), and could take more punishment than other Japanese Army fighters.

The Kawasaki Ki 45 Type 2 Twin-engine Fighter Toryu ("Nick") was another Japanese Army fighter the carrier Hellcat squadrons had not encountered before. Intended as a heavy fighter, the Toryu performed well as a ground attack and antishipping aircraft. Its top speed of 340mph was less than that of a Hellcat, but Hellcat pilots found the Toryu remarkably maneuverable and able to outclimb a Hellcat in steep climbs.

While the Army's bomber aircraft were seldom encountered in the air, the Mitsubishi Ki 46 Type 100 Command Reconnaissance Aircraft ("Dinah") played a much more important role. The Navy had to rely on the Army's Ki 46s for reconnaissance, which Navy pilots found disheartening. With a top speed of 375mph in the Ki 46-II and a range of 1,500 miles, the Dinah was an excellent reconnaissance aircraft, though without armor protection it caught fire easily when attacked.

During the September strikes on the Philippines, Japanese antiaircraft fire was more effective in shooting down American carrier aircraft than were Japanese fighters. Task Force 38 lost 12 aircraft in air combat, but 39 aircraft to antiaircraft guns. The Japanese Army and Navy relied on several types and calibers of antiaircraft guns to defend against enemy aircraft attacking at different altitudes. Calibers ranged from 7.7mm to 127mm. The Army and Navy used two weapons in the light antiaircraft category, the Model 92 7.7mm machine gun on a single mount, and the Model 93 13.2mm machine gun on a dual mount. In the medium antiaircraft category, the standard weapon was the Model 96 25mm cannon in a dual or triple mount which was most effective up to 1,000yds. The Model 88 75mm antiaircraft gun was the standard heavy antiaircraft weapon for defense of airfields and ground installations. The Army also used the earlier Model 14 105mm antiaircraft gun, while the Navy deployed the Type 10 120mm dual purpose antiaircraft and coastal defense gun. These heavy guns were often grouped together in emplacements located within a mile of an airfield, with light antiaircraft guns provided for defense against strafing aircraft. The lighter antiaircraft weapons used magazines instead of belts of ammunition, restricting their rate of fire.

The Japanese Army's Mitsubishi Ki-46 Type 100 Command Reconnaissance Aircraft performed valuable reconnaissance searching for the American task groups operating off the Philippines, much to the embarrassment of the Imperial Navy. (2008-3-31_Image_605_01, Peter M. Bowers Collection, Museum of Flight)

Targets and tactics

Under the *Sho* operations plans, the target for Japanese Army and Navy aircraft in the Philippines was the American invasion fleet in the area selected for the decisive battle, to be designated by IGHQ. The priority would be to destroy enemy aircraft carriers supporting the invasion. Once the carriers and their aircraft were eliminated, the next target would be the transport convoys carrying the invasion forces. If the enemy succeeded in landing troops, transports carrying reinforcements and troops already on land would take priority. IGHQ dictated a change in the air tactics to be employed in the decisive battle. Previously the Japanese had committed most of their aircraft to attacks on the enemy aircraft carriers as they launched preinvasion strikes to soften up the invasion area, but the losses incurred left too few airplanes for attacks on the invasion transports that followed. IGHQ now believed it would be more effective to attack with maximum strength during the third phase of an invasion, when attacks could be directed against the transports and the carriers. Army aircraft would attack transports and Navy aircraft the enemy carriers. To reduce losses from enemy attacks on air bases while waiting for the third phase of the invasion, air bases required strengthened installations and aircraft needed to be dispersed to other airfields.

In the first instance, reconnaissance aircraft had to locate the enemy carriers and the invasion fleet. With no unified command responsibility, reconnaissance was divided between the Navy and the Army as directed under the *Sho* operation agreement. Long-range patrols covering a distance of 600 to 900 miles off the Philippines became the responsibility of the First Air Fleet. Responsibility for shorter patrols out to a distance of 300 miles would be shared between the First Air Fleet and the Fourth Air Army through local agreement. For unknown reasons the CinC, Combined Fleet, dictated the specifics of the search missions, specifying that searches be carried out from Manila and Legaspi on Luzon, and from Davao on Mindanao, sending out five aircraft from Manila and nine aircraft from Davao to a distance of only 650 miles, though the search aircraft involved had longer ranges. The Navy apparently used G4M Betty bombers, P1Y1 Frances bombers, and D4Y Judy dive bombers for long-range searches, while relying on the Army's Ki-46 Dinah reconnaissance airplanes and Ki 45 Nick fighters for the shorter-range searches.

As the Navy had greater experience attacking enemy naval vessels, naval air units had responsibility for attacking the enemy carrier force employing land-based attack bombers and carrier dive bombers using conventional attack tactics, with possible assistance from the

The Imperial Navy's Type 96 25mm cannon had a vertical range of up to 14,000ft, covering enemy aircraft at low and medium altitudes. These could be in double or triple barrel mounts. (USMC 51806)

new Mitsubishi Ki 67 Type 4 Heavy Bomber ("Peggy") which could carry torpedoes as well as bombs. To attack transports the Army intended to use Type 1 and Type 3 fighters ("Oscar" and "Tony") armed with bombs, Type 2 Twin-engine fighters ("Nick"), Type 99 Assault Aircraft ("Sonia"), and Type 99 Light Bombers ("Lily"). The fighters would also be used to suppress antiaircraft fire. The Navy's older B5N Type 97 Carrier Attack planes ("Kate") and D3A Type 99 Carrier Bombers ("Val") would join in the attacks on transports. The plan was to withhold the main strength of the attack force until after any preliminary enemy carrier raids, dispersing air units to rear area bases until called upon to concentrate on the invasion force once it was committed.

Lacking adequate numbers of carrier dive bombers, the 201st Naval Air Group modified some of its A6M5 Zero-sen aircraft to carry a bomb under the fuselage and began training in what the Japanese called *Chohi Bakugeki*, referring to skip bombing, where the fighter would approach an enemy vessel flying 30–40ft above the sea and drop a bomb 400–600ft away, skipping the bomb into the side of the enemy ship. Similarly, the 761st Naval Air Group trained in night torpedo attacks in preparation for the *Sho* operation.

Air crews

The greatest problem facing the First Air Fleet and the 4th Air Army was the shortage of experienced pilots and crews. After sustaining severe losses during 1942 and 1943, the Army and Navy greatly expanded their pilot training, but shortages of instructors and training aircraft, particularly operational aircraft, produced pilots with less and less ability. The average number of flying hours steadily declined, from more than 700 hours at the start of the war in the Imperial Navy to less than 400 hours by the summer of 1944; Japanese Army Air Force pilots averaged even less.

The Imperial Navy had four categories of pilots: A class with over 1,000 flying hours; B class with between 400 and 1,000 hours; C class with less than 400 flying hours; and D class who had marginal ability to fly operational aircraft. In the 201st Naval Air Group, the Sento 305th Hikotai had 35 pilots, with just 12 rated A or B class, while in the Sento 306th

DEFENDER'S CAPABILITIES

Japanese Navy pilot trainees receive instruction in air combat tactics. As pilot losses mounted during the war the Imperial Navy was unable to provide an adequate number of instructor pilots with combat experience. (Author's collection)

Hikotai only two of 46 pilots were considered B class. It is highly likely that the Army air regiments had similar problems. The lack of experienced pilots made training that much more problematic. The results would show in the losses Japanese Army and Navy units suffered at the hands of American carrier pilots in the coming air battles.

Order of Battle: September 1944

US Navy

Commander Third Fleet: Admiral William F. Halsey, Jr
Task Force 38: Vice Admiral Marc A. Mitscher
Task Group 38.1: Vice Admiral John S. McCain
USS *Hornet* (CV-12) CVG-2
VF-2 37 F6F-3/5, F6F-3P/5P
VB-2 24 SB2C-3/12 F6F-5
VT-2 15 TBF-1C/TBM-1C
VFN-76 4 F6F-3N
USS *Wasp* (CV-18) CVG-14
VF-14 37 F6F-3/3P
VB-14 25 SB2C-3/10 F6F-3/5
VT-14 18 TBF-1C/TBM-1C, TBF-1D/TBM-1D
VFN-77 5 F6F-3N
USS *Belleau Wood* (CVL-24) CVLG-21
(September 6–17)
VF-21 23 F6F-5/5P
VT-21 9 TBM-1C

USS *Cowpens* (CVL-25) CVLG-22
VF-22 26 F6F-5/5P
VT-22 9 TBM-1C
USS *Monterey* (CVL-26) CVLG-28 (September 17–24)
VF-28 24 F6F-5/5P
VT-28 9 TBM-1C

Task Group 38.2: Rear Admiral Gerald F. Bogan
USS *Intrepid* (CV-11) CVG-18
VF-18 37 F6F-5/5P
VB-18 32 SB2C-3
VT-18 18 TBM-1C
VFN-78 4 F6F-3N
USS *Bunker Hill* (CV-17) CVG-8
VF-8 36 F6F-3/3P
VB-18 33 SB2C-1/SBF-1/SBW-1
VT-18 14 TBM-1C

VFN-76 4 F6F-3N
USS Cabot (CVL-28) CVLG-31
VF-31 24 F6F-5
VT-31 9 TBM-1C
USS Independence (CVL-22) CVLGN-41
VFN-41 19 F6F-3N/3/5
VTN-41 8 TBM-1D
Task Group 38.3: Rear Admiral Frederick C. Sherman
USS Essex (CV-9) CAG-15
VF-15 40 F6F-3/3P
VB-15 30 SB2C-1C
VT-15 20 TBF-1C/TBM-1C
VFN-77 4 F6F-3N
USS Lexington (CV-16) CVG-19
VF-19 37 F6F-3/3P
VB-19 36 SB2C-3
VT-19 18 TBM-1C
VFN-76 4 F6F-3N/2 TBM-1C
USS Princeton (CVL-23) CVLG-27
VF-27 25 F6F-3/5
VT-27 9 TBM-1C

USS Langley (CVL-27) CVLG-32
VF-32 21 F6F-3
VT-32 9 TBM-1C
Task Group 38.4: Rear Admiral Ralph E. Davison
USS Franklin (CV-13) CVG-13
VF-13 37 F6F-3/5/5P
VB-13 34 SB2C-3
VT-13 18 TBM-1C
VFN-77 3 F6F-3N
USS Enterprise (CV-6) CVG-20
VF-20 36 F6F-5
VB-13 34 SB2C-3
VT-13 19 TBM-1C
VFN-78 4 F6F-3N
USS San Jacinto (CVL-30) CVLG-51
VF-51 21 F6F-3/5
VT-51 7 TBM-1C
USS Belleau Wood (CVL-24) CVLG-21
(September 17–18)
VF-21 23 F6F-5/5P
VT-21 9 TBM-1C

Imperial Japanese Navy

First Air Fleet: Admiral Teraoka Kinpei
153rd Naval Air Group
Nakajima J1N1-S Night Fighter ("Irving")
Mitsubishi A6M5 Model 52 Type 0 Fighter ("Zeke")
201st Naval Air Group
Mitsubishi A6M5 Model 52 Type 0 Fighter ("Zeke")
761st Naval Air Group
Mitsubishi G4M Type 1 Attack Bomber ("Betty")
Yokosuka P1Y1 Navy Bomber ("Frances")
1021st Naval Air Group
Various transports

Imperial Japanese Army

Fourth Air Army: Lieutenant General Tominaga Kyoji
2nd Air Division
2nd Air Regiment
Mitsubishi Ki-46 Type 100 Command Reconnaissance Aircraft ("Dinah")
6th Air Brigade
65th Air Regiment
Mitsubishi Ki-51 Type 99 Assault Aircraft ("Sonia")
66th Air Regiment
Mitsubishi Ki-51 Type 99 Assault Aircraft ("Sonia")
7th Air Brigade
12th Air Regiment
Mitsubishi Ki-21 Type 97 Heavy Bomber ("Sally")
62nd Air Regiment
Nakajima Ki-49-II Type 100 Heavy Bomber ("Helen")

10th Air Brigade
45th Air Regiment
Kawasaki Ki-45 Type 2 Twin-engine Fighter ("Nick")
13th Air Brigade
30th Air Regiment
Nakajima Ki-43 Type 1 Fighter ("Oscar")
31st Air Regiment
Nakajima Ki-43 Type 1 Fighter ("Oscar")
22nd Air Brigade
17th Air Regiment
Kawasaki Ki-61 Type 3 Fighter ("Tony")
19th Air Regiment
Kawasaki Ki-61 Type 3 Fighter ("Tony")

CAMPAIGN OBJECTIVES
First steps in the Philippines

American plans and objectives

USMC LVTs approach the beach at Peleliu on September 15, 1944. The American objective was to seize the Palau Islands to guard General MacArthur's right flank as his forces advanced west toward the Philippines. (80G-59498, RG80, NARA)

The immediate objective of the September 1944 carrier strikes on the Philippines was to prevent Japanese air power from interfering with the landings on Peleliu and Morotai, both scheduled for September 15. The longer-term objective was to maximize damage to Japanese military forces and capabilities in the Philippines in preparation for operations against Mindanao and Leyte planned for later in the year.

The Palau Islands and Morotai were the last barriers on the way to the Philippines. Their capture would provide bases for American land-based aircraft to attack the Philippines. Palau, the westernmost island in the Caroline Islands, lay some 900 miles from recently captured Guam and 540 miles from Davao on Mindanao. It had been an important staging stop for Japanese aircraft flying from the Marianas to the South Pacific via Ulithi Atoll and the island of Yap to the northeast of Palau. Capturing the Palau Islands would give the US Navy control over approaches to the Philippines through the Western Pacific, and would protect the right flank of General MacArthur's forces in the Southwest Pacific in their advance to Morotai. The invasion plan, Operation *Stalemate II*, called for landings on two of the islands, Peleliu and Angaur, which had fewer Japanese troops. The Navy planned landings on Yap and Ulithi for October 5, 1944, after securing the Palau Islands. The air bases on Mindanao were the closest bases to Palau that could pose a threat to the invasion, with the possibility of obtaining reinforcements from other bases in the Philippines. Still, at a range of 500 miles or more from Mindanao, it was considered unlikely that any airplanes other than twin-engine bombers could attack the invasion force. The number of bombers available to the Japanese on Mindanao was estimated to be around 30, but there were possibly 100 more at central and northern Philippines bases, but overall the threat to Palau from air attack was thought to be limited.

Japanese aircraft on Mindanao, however, did pose a potential threat to the landings on Morotai. General MacArthur wanted to capture a position in between the Vogelkop Peninsula in eastern New Guinea and Mindanao that could provide air bases to defend the left flank on

On September 15, 1944, American forces landed on Morotai, close to Halmahera, the largest island in the Moluccas in what was then the Netherlands East Indies. Task Force 38's mission was to prevent the Japanese from interfering with the landings at Morotai and Palau. (80G-282601, RG80, NARA)

his approach to Mindanao, which he intended to invade in November, against Japanese air attack and to provide air support for the invasion. MacArthur initially considered landings on Halmahera, the largest island in the Moluccas, but as the Japanese maintained a strong garrison on Halmahera, MacArthur chose to invade the island of Morotai, 25 miles off the northern coast of Halmahera. MacArthur wanted the Fast Carrier Task Force to neutralize the Mindanao airfields before the landings on Morotai, designated Operation *Tradewind*. To preserve surprise, MacArthur wanted no strikes on Morotai before the landings, but requested that one Fast Carrier group strike Japanese airfields in the northern Celebes on the morning of September 15, and to remain in the area to provide cover for the invasion against Japanese air attacks from the Celebes.

The Japanese had airfields located across Mindanao, but it was believed that the cluster of airfields around Davao, as well as shipping that might be in Davao harbor, would be profitable targets. CincPac scheduled Task Force 38 to carry out strikes against Mindanao on September 9 and 10. As MacArthur had not requested the Fast Carriers to strike Morotai before the landings on September 15, Task Force 38 would be free to carry out additional strikes on Mindanao.

The overall objective for Admiral Halsey's Third Fleet was "to gain and maintain control of the eastern approaches to the Philippines and the Formosa-China Coast area" by capturing Peleliu, and later Yap and Ulithi. The general task of all CincPac forces involved was to "maintain and extend unremitting military pressure against Japan. Apply maximum attrition to enemy air, ground, and naval forces by all possible means in all areas." This applied particularly to the Japanese fleet. Nimitz included in his instructions to Admiral Halsey

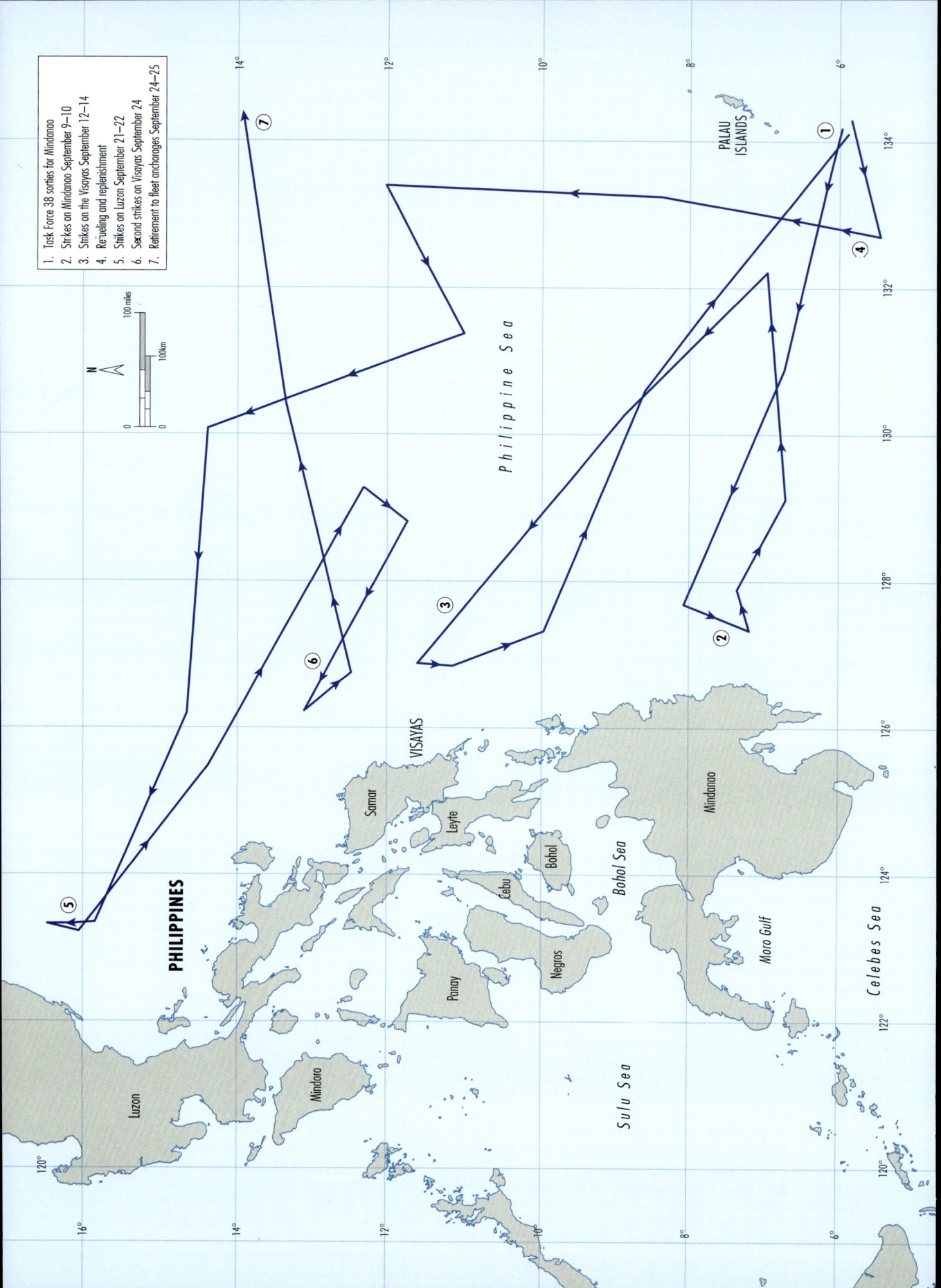

OPPOSITE TRACK OF TASK FORCE 38 DURING CARRIER STRIKES ON THE PHILIPPINES

an additional objective, "to utilize every opportunity which may be presented or created to destroy major portions of the enemy fleet."

Task Force 38 now became the Covering Force for the Palau and Morotai operations, helping cover the landings and striking at Japanese air bases on Mindanao. The operations plan called for Task Force 38 to strike targets in the Palaus on September 6 and 7, then sail for Mindanao to neutralize Japanese air power on the island, with strikes against airfields from September 9 to September 14. Following the Mindanao strikes, Task Force 38 would become available to cover the landings on Peleliu on September 15. Nimitz recognized the risk of sending the Fast Carriers to conduct sustained attacks on Japanese land-based air power, a mission the Fast Carriers had never undertaken before, but he thought the risk acceptable if it created an opportunity to attack the Japanese fleet. Even if the attacks did not result in a fleet engagement, they would conform to the overall objective of inflicting maximum attrition on the Japanese in the Philippines.

Halsey considered the tasks laid out for Third Fleet and Task Force 38 in light of the larger tasks assigned to CincPac. Always aggressively minded, Halsey considered the schedule of operations to pertain more to logistical planning. He wanted to maintain the mobility and flexibility of his striking force to ensure that the Fast Carriers could exploit any enemy weaknesses that arose.

The basic plan, proven in previous operations, was to approach the target area by night to achieve surprise. To obtain air superiority over the target area, the carriers would launch a dawn fighter sweep. Attacks from all three task groups would follow the fighter sweep, spaced at intervals until the task groups withdrew from the area. Task Force 38 divided Mindanao into separate areas so that each task group could concentrate its efforts in a single area. Task Group 38.3's targets were the airfields in central and northern Mindanao, with Task Groups 38.1 and 38.2 taking on Davao and the airfields in the southern part of the island where the strike forces were expected to meet the heaviest opposition.

Japanese plans and objectives

From the end of July 1944 the requirements of the *Sho* operations dictated Japanese plans and objectives. The foundation of the *Sho* operation was the decision that whichever one of the inner defense areas – the Philippines, Formosa and the Ryukyus, the Home Islands, or northern Japan – was the focus of the main strength of the enemy would be designated the decisive battle theater, and all available forces would be concentrated in that location to defeat the enemy. Imperial General Headquarters in Tokyo would determine when and where to activate the respective *Sho* operation.

Under the July 24, 1944 agreement between the Army and Navy covering plans for *Sho Operation No. 1* over the Philippines, the Army and Navy were to complete their preparations by August 1944 and in the event of an enemy invasion to commit all their forces in a coordinated effort to destroy the enemy. The Navy agreed to concentrate the First Air Fleet and the Second Air Fleet (rebuilding in Japan) to the Philippines, while the Army agreed to send two fighter and one heavy bomber regiment drawn from training units, one fighter, one light bomber, and one heavy bomber regiment from the 8th Air Division on Formosa, and two fighter regiments from the Fifth Air Army in China.

The agreement laid down basic operating procedures for the decisive battle. Before the start of the decisive battle, the seemingly contradictory objective was to destroy the enemy's fighting power while minimizing Japanese losses. Aircraft were to be dispersed in depth and

Japanese antiaircraft fire accounted for more Task Force 38 aircraft downed than Japanese aircraft. Japanese airfields had multiple types of antiaircraft weapons to take on attacking aircraft at different altitudes, beginning with the heavy Type 88 75mm cannon organized in batteries of multiple guns. The shell from a Type 88 could reach up to 29,000ft. (Author's collection)

defense of air bases was to be provided by antiaircraft weapons instead of aircraft. In the decisive battle against an invasion force, the Army and Navy were to utilize their entire air strength in day and night attacks against enemy carriers and transports.

On July 26 the Navy section of IGHQ issued its own directive for the *Sho* operation relating to the Philippines. The directive instructed Navy units in the Philippines to prepare bases that could accommodate the entire strength of the First and Second Air Fleets, primarily in the Clark Field complex on Luzon and the airfields around Bacolod on Negros. The Navy air forces would concentrate on destroying enemy carriers, then work jointly with the Navy's surface forces to destroy transports involved in the invasion and conveying reinforcements.

The *Sho-1* directives presented the air commanders in the Philippines with a dilemma. Air units preparing for the *Sho* operation were not to commit their forces to countering preinvasion attacks. They were to conserve their strength for attacks on the enemy when the actual invasion had been launched. How then were they to defend their air bases against enemy attack?

THE CAMPAIGN

The carriers move in

Preliminary actions, August 28 to September 8, 1944

As a diversion from the upcoming invasion of the Palau Islands, and to inflict further damage against Japanese installations that could interfere with the invasion, Admiral Halsey ordered Task Group 38.4 (USS *Franklin*, USS *Enterprise*, and USS *San Jacinto*) to carry out strikes on Iwo Jima and Chichi Jima in the Bonins, and Yap and Ulithi in the Carolines before taking over responsibility for preinvasion strikes on the Palaus from the rest of Task Force 38. Task Group 38.4 sortied from Eniwetok at 0545hrs on August 28, 1944, arriving at a point some 140–160 miles away from Iwo Jima and Chichi Jima at midday on August 31. En route the carrier air groups carried out training exercises.

Shortly after midday on August 31, the *Franklin* launched a fighter sweep comprising 29 F6F-5 Hellcats from VF-13, half equipped with rockets, to destroy any Japanese aircraft around Iwo Jima. VF-13 flew a sweep around the island, but finding no aircraft returned to Iwo to attack the airfields on the island. As the formation came on Airfield No. 1, the pilots saw ten aircraft taking off from the field and immediately attacked, claiming eight Zekes, one Kate (Nakajima B5N), and a Dinah shot down. The Hellcats then turned to strafing parked aircraft on Airfields No. 1 and No. 2, claiming ten destroyed and a further 18 damaged. Leaving the airfields, VF-13 strafed several small cargo vessels, sinking one and forcing another to the beach. That night an F6F-3N from VFN-77 shot down an H8K2 Emily flying boat searching for the Task Group.

During the following two days, September 1 and 2, the *Franklin*'s CVG-13 carried out eight strikes against Iwo Jima, one every two and a half hours. The strike groups comprised a mixed force of F6F Hellcats, SB2C Helldivers, and TBM Avengers. The Hellcats strafed targets with their machine guns and rockets, while the SB2Cs dropped 1,000lb bombs, and the TBMs a mix of 2,000lb, 1,000lb, and 500lb bombs, hitting installations on the airfields. On the first day's strikes Japanese antiaircraft fire shot down one TBM, but the crew were rescued. Two Hellcat pilots who had carried out a photographic sortie after the last strike on September 2 returned to the *Franklin* reporting that they had found a group

An SB2C Helldiver heads back to the carriers after the last strike of the day on Cebu town. Smoke billows up from hits on shipping in the harbor and the dock areas. (80G-247516, RG80, NARA)

of camouflaged Japanese aircraft at a newly built airfield on the north end of Iwo Jima. VF-13 flew a hurriedly organized fighter sweep with 19 Hellcats carrying incendiary clusters. The pilots returned to the carrier ten minutes before sunset claiming to have destroyed 14 Zekes, two Hamps, and eight twin-engine aircraft.

Enterprise and *San Jacinto* carried out strikes against Chichi Jima. On August 31, while *San Jacinto*'s VF-51 flew combat air patrols over the two carriers, 28 F6F-5 Hellcats from VF-20 and 12 SB2C-3 Helldivers from *Enterprise* carried out a sweep over Chichi Jima and nearby Haha Jima, hitting naval installations and the seaplane base at Futami Bay on Chichi Jima. Several of the SB2C-3s carried the Douglas DGP-1 gunpack, used in combat for the first time. Antiaircraft fire shot down one Helldiver, but the pilot made a water landing off the coast and he and his gunner were rescued. During September 1 and 2, the *Enterprise* and *San Jacinto* air groups launched strikes against targets on Chichi Jima and Haha Jima, as well as shipping in the area. On the second strike of the day on September 1, VB-20 lost another SB2C-3 and crew to heavy antiaircraft fire. The next day VF-20 lost an F6F-5P to antiaircraft fire while on a photo run, but the pilot made a successful water landing and was rescued by a submarine. VT-51 was less fortunate, losing a TBM to antiaircraft fire, two of the crew bailing out but only the pilot surviving. After completing the strikes on Iwo Jima and Chichi Jima, Task Group 38.4 returned to Saipan for replenishment.

Machine guns could put up a stream of fire against low-flying aircraft. This wartime news photo shows a dual mounting for the 12.7mm Type 1 machine gun normally mounted in aircraft like the Ki-43 and the Ki-61. (Author's collection)

Task Group 38.4 sailed for Yap from Saipan on September 5, arriving at a point 200 miles from Yap the next day in the afternoon. *Enterprise* and *Franklin* carried out fighter sweeps over Yap, while later in the afternoon VF-51 from the *San Jacinto* sent four Hellcats on a photo mission to cover the island. While the *Franklin*'s VF-13 fighter sweep was uneventful, the *Enterprise*'s VF-20 lost three Hellcats, one to antiaircraft fire and two in a possible midair collision while diving on a target on the island. Over the next two days the carriers conducted several attacks on Yap and Ulithi, but Yap in particular had been so badly damaged by B-24s from the Seventh Air Force that further strikes were cancelled. Task Group 38.4 set off for Palau on September 9 to provide preinvasion strikes against Palau, taking over from Task Groups 38.1, 38.2, and 38.3.

The other three task groups had sortied from Eniwetok on August 29 for the Palau Islands, arriving at a point 150 miles southeast of the islands on September 6. At 1300hrs, USS *Wasp* sent off 32 Hellcats from VF-14 on a fighter sweep over Angaur and Ngesebus islands in the Palau group, encountering no enemy aircraft. Over the next two days aircraft from the three task groups carried out strikes against targets on several islands, hitting airfield installations, antiaircraft positions, fuel dumps, and docks. The islands had already received so much damage from previous carrier and land-based air attacks that further strikes were deemed

Preparing to load a Mk 13 torpedo on an Avenger on board USS *Wasp* (CV-18). The TBM Avengers could carry a single torpedo, but more often carried four 500lb bombs in the bomb bay for glide bombing attacks. (80G-298609, RG80, NARA)

unnecessary. On the night of September 8 the three task groups sailed for Mindanao and the first carrier strikes against the Philippines and against Japanese land-based air power.

The strikes on Mindanao, September 9–10, 1944

Allied Intelligence believed that the Japanese had nearly 200 aircraft based on Mindanao. The Japanese had nine major airfields and numerous smaller airfields scattered around the island. There was every expectation that Task Force 38's attack on Mindanao would meet strong opposition. Aircraft and airfields were the priority targets. During the night of September 8 Task Force 38's three task groups steamed toward Mindanao at 25kts, arriving at a position 50 to 75 miles from the island by the early morning of September 9. The initial fighter sweeps took off that morning.

At 0550hrs, shortly before sunrise, Task Group 38.3 sent off a fighter sweep to cover the airfields on northern Mindanao composed of 16 F6F-3 Hellcats from VF-15 off USS *Essex* and 16 F6F-3/5 from VF-19 aboard USS *Lexington*, with Cdr David McCampbell, commanding CVG-15, as the sweep leader. To their surprise, the pilots encountered no aerial opposition, though VF-15 shot down a single Mitsubishi Ki-57 Army Type 100 Transport (possibly the Navy version L4M1 Type 0 Transport, both designated "Topsy") and two D3A Vals that appeared to be unaware of the attacking carrier aircraft. VF-19 covered the airfields in the southern part of the northern sector assigned to TG38.3, but by agreement with VF-15 flew on to the northern part of the sector when the southern airfields turned up empty. At Lumbia, Cagayan, and Del Monte airfields VF-19 found aircraft on the ground.

Cdr David McCampbell, right, Carrier Air Group Commander of Air Group 15 on the *Essex*, with Lt Cdr James Rigg, CO of VF-15, with VF-15's score board in early August 1944. Early on September 9, McCampbell led a fighter sweep with Hellcats from VF-15 and VF-19 over the airfields on northern Mindanao. (80G-237480, RG80, NARA)

Clouds covering the airfield at Lumbia cleared just as the Hellcats came over to reveal 15 twin-engine airplanes. Diving down from 5,000ft the Hellcats made repeated runs setting all 15 aircraft on fire. At Cagayan the squadron claimed three twin-engine and three single-engine airplanes destroyed, and six twin-engine airplanes at Del Monte.

Task Force 38.3's first strike of the day took off shortly after the carriers launched the fighter sweep. CVG-15 sent 15 Hellcats from VF-15, 12 VB-15 Helldivers, and nine VT-15 Avengers, with CVG-19 providing 15 VB-19 Helldivers, and nine VT-19 Avengers. CVLG-32 from USS *Langley* added 12 Hellcats from VF-32 and nine Avengers from VT-32, while VF-27 off USS *Princeton* flew combat air patrols over the task group. Airfields in the Del Monte were the target for CVG-15 and the Valencia areas for CVG-19 and CVLG-32. Because of clouds over Del Monte, VB-15 and VT-15 attacked Lumbia and Cagayan airfields, where they damaged airfield buildings and VT-15 claimed five single-engine airplanes destroyed. The VF-15 divisions escorted the bombers to their targets, catching one more poor Topsy flying at 13,000ft which was promptly shot down. After strafing the airfields, the VF-15 Hellcats were escorting the bombers back to the *Essex* when they sighted a convoy of 35 small coastal freighters off the east coast of Mindanao. Seven Hellcats continued to escort the bombers, while four peeled off to strafe the convoy, calling out the convoy's location to Cdr McCampbell and the other VF-15 divisions on the fighter sweep. The first VF-15 division to attack claimed four ships sunk and eight left burning. The Hellcats on the fighter sweep claimed seven more sunk and 24 damaged, losing one F6F when the pilot flew over the ship he was strafing just as its load of ammunition blew up. Later, Admiral Halsey gave permission to Task Group 38.3 to send two cruisers and four destroyers to add to the destruction.

CVG-15 made three more strikes against targets in northern Mindanao that day, but after hitting barrack buildings at the airfields soon found a lack of other worthwhile targets so turned to attacking shipping and harbor facilities at Surigao on the northern tip of the island. On the third strike of the day a section from VF-15 surprised a Ki-46 Dinah and shot it down, the only Japanese aircraft VF-15 encountered after the morning's attack. The Helldivers and Avengers attacked ships and dock areas with bombs and rockets. One

Finding no worthwhile targets on the airfields around northern Mindanao, Air Group 15 went after shipping in Surigao on the island's northern coast. Firing rockets, VT-15 claimed one freighter sunk and another seriously damaged with help from VF-15's Hellcats who strafed and bombed the ships with 500lb bombs. (Carrier Air Group 15 Action Report for September 9, 1944, RG38, NARA)

Helldiver was hit hard by antiaircraft fire but got back to the task group to make a water landing near a destroyer.

CVG-19 and CVLG-32 had similar results in strikes against their assigned airfields, the fighters going down to strafe and the dive bombers and torpedo bombers hitting barracks and other buildings around the airfields. VF-32 provided high cover for the bombers and the other fighters. The strikes encountered no enemy aircraft in the air, and saw none on the ground. After each attack a Hellcat flew over the field to take photographs. With no suitable targets at the airfields, on the last two strikes of the day the strike forces turned to attacking shipping and hitting harbor installations in northern Mindanao. The next day VF-15 claimed a Dinah and an Irving shot down on an early fighter sweep, while VF-19 shot down a Val as the Japanese aircraft approached one of the Del Monte airfields for a landing. Escorting the first strike mission of the day, VF-15 claimed another Dinah. The two Task Group 38.3 air groups, joined on this day by VF-27 and VT-27 from the *Princeton*, hit the airfields in northern Mindanao again, and attacked shipping, but with a dearth of targets Task Force 38 cancelled the rest of the strikes scheduled for September 10.

Task Groups 38.1 and 38.2 followed the same operational plan in their strikes on southern Mindanao. Task Group 38.1's assignment was to strike the airfields around Davao, at Digos across the Davao Gulf, and around Sarangani Bay at the southern tip of Mindanao. The morning of September 9 began with VF-14 from USS *Wasp* making a fighter sweep over Davao Gulf with 19 Hellcats. Contrary to expectations, the sweep was uneventful, encountering no Japanese aircraft. The fighters took photos of several of the airfields around the Gulf and strafed a radar station at the tip of Cape San Augustin. USS *Cabot* sent 16 F6F-5s from VF-22 on a Target Combat Air Patrol over Sarangani Bay. Finding no Japanese aircraft, the Hellcats strafed six small Fox Tare Dog freighters (700–1,300 gross tons) leaving four sunk and two seriously damaged and beached.

Shortly thereafter *Wasp* launched its first strike of the day against Padada airfield near Digos, sending eight SB2C-3 Helldivers and two F6F-3 fighter bombers from VB-14, with an escort of six VF-14 Hellcats each carrying a single 500lb bomb. Another VB-14 Helldiver went along to photograph the results of the strike. USS *Hornet* sent off its first strike around the same time, 12 SB2C-3s from VB-2 with nine TBM-1Cs from VT-2 with an escort of 20 F6Fs from VF-2. The *Hornet* strike joined up with the *Wasp* strike force, with the *Hornet* force leading the attack. The *Cowpens*'s CVLG-22 also participated in the strike on Padada, eight Hellcats of VF-22 escorting eight Avengers of VT-22. En route the strike force received word from the fighter sweep that there was no air opposition. The Japanese radar station at Cape San Augustin picked up the approaching carrier aircraft on radar and sent out a warning, but owing to communications problems the warning didn't arrive until the American aircraft were over Davao and closing in on the airfield.

As the dive bombers began their dive on the airfield, Japanese antiaircraft guns opened up, the fire intensifying as the attack continued. Just before the bombers began their attack, Hellcats from VF-2, VF-14, and VF-22 went down to strafe antiaircraft positions around the airfield, VF-22 adding rockets to their .50 caliber machine-gun fire. VF-22 claimed two airplanes destroyed in strafing attacks across the airfield. The VB-2 and VT-2 bombers hit heavy antiaircraft gun positions and buildings around the airfield, while VB-14 and VT-22 added to the damage. VB-14's Hellcat fighter bombers made strafing runs across the airfield hitting what appeared to be parked aircraft, though later photographic coverage determined that these were dummy aircraft. The second strike of the morning saw aircraft from *Hornet* and *Wasp* hit the airfield at Buayan at the north end of Sarangani Bay. VB-2 sent ten SB2C-3s and seven F6F-5 fighter bombers, with VB-14 adding 11 SB2C-3s. The dive bombers hit buildings on the airfield, VB-2's aircraft demolishing a large hangar building with 1,000lb bombs. The seven Hellcat fighter bombers went to search for an airfield reported nearby at the town of Makar, but finding no airfield there bombed the town and sampans along the shore.

VF-22 off USS *Cowpens* (CVL-25) claimed two aircraft destroyed on an airfield near the town of Padada, southwest of Davao. One of the squadron's F6F-5 is shown here taking off from the *Cowpens* during the September strikes. (80G-291216, RG80, NARA)

While *Hornet*, *Wasp*, and *Cabot* aircraft carried out the strikes on Mindanao on September 9, USS *Belleau Wood* had responsibility for maintaining combat air patrols over Task Group 38.1. Now alert to enemy aircraft carriers off the coast of Mindanao, the Japanese Navy and Army sent aircraft out to determine their location. At 0839hrs *Belleau Wood*'s radar detected a bogey approaching the task group and vectored a division of VF-21 Hellcats to intercept. The Hellcats approached the Japanese aircraft, which they identified as a Frances (P1Y1), with a 4,000ft altitude advantage. Diving to attack, the division leader flamed the port engine, while his wingman made an attack from the rear. The Frances returned fire ineffectively from its flexible 20mm rear gun. The four Hellcat pilots made two more runs, setting the starboard wing of the Frances on fire. The Frances rolled over on its back and went down into the sea, the pilot bailing out. Shortly thereafter *Belleau Wood* picked up another bogey and sent a division to intercept. Flying at 10,000ft the division found the bogey 3,000ft above them and identified the Japanese airplane as a Nick twin-engine fighter (Ki-45). The Nick outclimbed the Hellcats until they had reached 22,000ft where the Hellcats engaged their high blower for more power. The Nick entered heavy clouds, one section of the division losing contact. The wingman of the other section also lost contact, but on entering a shallow dive and descending saw the Nick diving steeply with a Hellcat on its tail, flown by the section leader. The wingman and the pilots of the other section saw the Nick crash into the sea, with the pursuing Hellcat crashing seconds later.

With a lack of worthwhile targets at the airfields around southern Mindanao, Task Group 38.1 ordered some of its air groups north to attack Japanese shipping in the Cagayan area in the third strike of the day. VT-2 went after shipping in Cagayan harbor, four Avengers dropping torpedoes which ran erratically, but one managed to hit a small freighter at the dock while another hit the dock itself causing a large explosion and fire. On the way to Cagayan two sections of VB-2 Helldivers hit two freighters in the harbor at Nasipit near Cagayan, claiming to have sunk both ships. Seeing no ships in Cagayan harbor, the third VB-2 section bombed buildings at Cagayan airfield. Nine Helldivers from VB-14 with seven Hellcat fighter bombers had also been ordered to attack shipping in Cagayan harbor, but when *Hornet*'s CVG-2 went after these ships VB-14 bombed the Cagayan airfield instead. The Helldivers bombed buildings on the airfield starting two large fires, while two of the fighter bomber pilots strafed two Bettys (G4M) found on the airfield, setting one of the two on fire. Task Group 38.1's final strike of the day was a return to Padada airfield near Digos, where VB-14 bombed concentrations of antiaircraft guns along with VT-14's Avengers and Hellcats, which made strafing runs on the antiaircraft positions.

Task Group 38.2, given the area around Davao city, sent 16 Hellcats from VF-18 off the *Intrepid* and 16 Hellcats from the *Bunker Hill*'s VF-8 on a fighter sweep over Davao before the first strike of the day. The fighters saw no aircraft in the air over the area, but VF-8 pilots saw a Judy (D4Y) taking off from Davao II airfield. One division dived down to attack as the Judy fled out to sea, promptly shooting it down. The sweep continued to Santa Cruz airfield near Davao where the fighters dropped down to strafe parked aircraft which appeared to be dummies.

While USS *Cabot* maintained combat air patrols over the carriers and their escort vessels, during the day Task Group 38.2 sent off five strikes to attack airfields around Davao. The *Intrepid*'s CVG-18 made four strikes against Matina airfield just next to Davao. On the first strike 15 SB2C-3s from VB-18 dropped 1,000lb bombs on the runway and revetments, while four TBM-1Cs from VT-18 dropped 2,000lb bombs on the runway and on antiaircraft positions, and four others hit the revetment area with 100lb fragmentation bombs. CVG-8 from *Bunker Hill* sent 12 SB2C-1C and eight TBF-1C to attack Davao I airfield with an escort of 21 VF-8 Hellcats, hitting the runway and revetment areas. CVG-18 sent out three more strikes, one to Daliao airfield and two back to Matina, the Helldivers and Avengers using the same mix of 1,000lb and 2,000lb bombs against runways, revetments, and buildings on the airfields. CVG-8 sent its next strike to bomb Licanan airfield near Davao, hitting the runway and buildings, followed by three more strikes against Davao I. On the second strike against Davao I, antiaircraft fire shot down an SB2C-1C, the two crewmen bailing out near the airfield. The final strikes hit the runways, a power house, and antiaircraft positions around the airfield.

Task Force 38 had scheduled Task Groups 38.1 and 38.2 to carry out a fighter sweep and four more strikes over southern Mindanao on September 10, but after completing the sweep and the first two strikes, Task Force 38 cancelled the remaining two strikes due to the

During the September strikes on the Philippines, Vought OS2U Kingfishers flying from battleships and cruisers rescued several downed aircrew in waters close to shore. (80G-283564, RG80, NARA)

lack of targets. During the fighter sweep VF-18 shot down a Dinah, and claimed a Betty, Val, and Zeke destroyed on the ground at Matina airfield, with three twin-engine and one single-engine aircraft probably destroyed. Aircraft from the *Intrepid, Bunker Hill,* and *Cabot* bombed warehouses, oil storage tanks, and dock facilities in the Davao port area, starting large fires. After recovering the aircraft from the second strike, Task Groups 38.1 and 38.2 headed east to rendezvous with the fleet tankers the next day.

Ironically, that morning a lookout posted to watch the entrance to Davao Gulf thought large waves at the entrance to the Gulf were the wakes of landing craft and transmitted a report. As the report moved up the chain of command it became exaggerated stating that enemy amphibious tanks were approaching Davao II airfield. The report was flashed to the Imperial Navy high command without verification and before it could be rescinded the Commander-in-Chief of the Combined Fleet issued an order to prepare for *Sho Operation No. 1*, which then had to be cancelled to the embarrassment of the Navy.

In two days of strikes on Mindanao, Task Force 38 had carried out 1,428 sorties, dropped 485 tons of bombs – almost all against airfields – and claimed 14 Japanese aircraft shot down and 44 destroyed on the ground, fewer than expected. There had been more damage to Japanese shipping, with eight small freighters and 52 small craft claimed sunk and 68 damaged, but the lack of additional worthwhile targets did not justify continuing strikes against Mindanao until September 14 as scheduled. The cost to Task Force 38 of the attacks on Mindanao amounted to six F6F Hellcats, two SB2C Helldivers, and one TBM Avenger lost in combat. It was clear from the small number of aircraft encountered on the main airfields on Mindanao and their limited facilities that the threat to the landings on Palau and Morotai from Japanese air power on the island was no longer a concern.

What was unexpected was the lack of Japanese reaction to the carrier strikes. No Japanese aircraft rose up to counter the marauding carrier aircraft nor did any aircraft attack the task groups cruising off the coast of Mindanao. The impression was of weakness. Confident that the fleet supporting the landings on Palau, with Task Group 38.4 also available, would be more than adequate to cover the landings, Admiral Halsey decided to cancel the scheduled additional days of strikes on Mindanao and instead attack Japanese air power in the Visaya Island group in the central Philippines where there might well be richer pickings for his carriers. His decision conformed to Admiral Nimitz's general orders to seek a fleet engagement with the Imperial Navy and to inflict maximum attrition on Japanese forces. What Halsey did not know was that the Japanese could well have attacked his carriers but chose not to. The *Sho* operation demanded that Japanese forces conserve their strength for the decisive battle and not commit their air units against raids ahead of the main invasion.

The strikes on the Visayas, September 12–14, 1944

The Visayas are a group of islands located in the central region of the Philippines archipelago. The main islands are, from east to west, Samar, Leyte, Bohol, Cebu, Negros, and Panay. The Japanese Army and Navy had established numerous operational airfields in the Visayas, particularly on Cebu and Negros. After retiring from Mindanao on September 10, Admiral Halsey informed his task groups that their next targets would be airfields and shipping in the Visayas. He allocated specific target areas to each task group as follows:

Task Group 38.1: Cebu and Negros.
Task Group 38.2: Leyte, Samar, and Bulan (southern Luzon).
Task Group 38.3: Cebu, Negros, and Bohol.

Since the targets on Cebu, Negros, and Panay were located at the edge of the normal range for carrier aircraft, the task groups had to arrange launches around the return of previous

Shipping and harbor installations around the town of Cebu came under sustained attack on September 12, the first day of the strikes against the Visayas. Smoke rises from bombs dropped in the harbor area while another bomb has just missed a large freighter to the lower left of the photograph. (80G-247510, RG80, NARA)

strikes, which meant launching fewer strikes during the day. On September 11 all three task groups refueled from fleet tankers and received replacement aircraft setting course later in the day for the initial launching point for the Visaya strikes 40–60 miles east of the southern tip of Samar.

Task Group 38.2 sent off a fighter sweep at 0615hrs on the morning of September 12 to cover airfields on Samar, Leyte, and Bulan at the southern tip of Luzon. USS *Bunker Hill* contributed eight VF-8 Hellcats to the fighter sweep, joining eight from VF-18, and eight from VF-31. Naval Intelligence had reports of 13 airfields on Leyte and four on Samar. The fighter sweep found no Japanese aircraft airborne, and only six airfields on Leyte and one on Samar; the airfield on Bulan was flooded. The task group sent off two strikes against the airfields on Leyte with aircraft from CVG-8, CVG-18, and CVLG-31. The first strike claimed a Zeke destroyed at Dulag airfield and two at Mojon. VB-8 and VT-8 claimed three unidentified single-engine aircraft destroyed at Tacloban with bombs and rockets. The Helldivers and Avengers dropped 100lb and 500lb bombs, cratering runways and hitting several buildings at several airfields; VT-31 dropped two 2,000lb "daisy cutters" set to go off on contact with the ground. The strikes returned to the carriers reporting no significant targets on any of the airfields. Instead, Admiral Halsey instructed Task Group 38.2 to send its third strike to attack Lahug airfield near the city of Cebu.

Arriving near Cebu city, the CVG-18 strike force found Lahug covered in cloud, so attacked shipping in Cebu city harbor. VB-18 and VT-18 dropped 100lb and 500lb bombs on several ships, claiming one large Sugar Able freighter sunk and another left sinking, with two smaller freighters sunk and five believed to be sinking. By the time CVG-8 arrived, Cebu city was closed in with cloud, but the air group found seven freighters at the northern tip of Cebu and attacked. Five VB-8 SB2C-3s attacked a Fox Tare Baker freighter estimated at 8,000 gross tons with 500lb bombs. VT-8 came in shortly after, dropping more 500lb bombs, the last pilot in the TBM division dropping his bombs in salvo hitting astern. On fire, the ship began to settle in the water when there was a large explosion and the ship sank. VB-8 and VT-8 sank one more freighter and left two more seriously damaged. Two divisions from VF-31 found a small freighter and severely damaged the ship by skip bombing, forcing the ship to beach to prevent sinking. The fourth strike of the day claimed more ships sunk

An SB2C Helldiver pulls up after dive bombing an oil tanker near the Cebu docks. Five bombs have hit near the ship. (Task Group 38.1 Action Report for September 12, 1944, RG38, NARA)

and damaged, the Hellcats of VF-18 claiming 12 small ships sunk through strafing attacks. During the day Hellcat night fighters from VFN-41 shot down a Betty bomber and a Dinah reconnaissance aircraft likely searching for the American carriers.

Having had few encounters with Japanese aircraft over Mindanao, the early morning fighter sweeps and later airfield strikes on Cebu and Negros from Task Groups 38.1 and 38.3 ran into a storm of opposition from Japanese fighters, the carrier fighter squadrons ending the day with claims for over 100 Japanese aircraft destroyed, probably destroyed, or damaged in air combat. The rumors of American forces preparing to land on Mindanao that came out on September 10 induced the 201st Naval Air Group to send 89 Zero-sen fighters from Manila to Cebu, but when the rumor turned out to be incorrect, roughly half the aircraft returned to Manila.

The Japanese Army had the 30th and 31st Fighter Regiments based at Bacolod airfield on Negros. Once again it took an excessive amount of time to get information from Japanese radar stations to the air units on Cebu and Negros. The Hellcats from Task Group 38.1 and 38.3 arrived over Cebu with no warning.

Heavy rain delayed the launch of the fighter sweep over Cebu until 0800hrs. Task Group 38.3 launched 16 Hellcats, eight from VF-15 and eight from VF-19 with the commander of VF-19 leading the sweep. Arriving over Cebu city and nearby Mactan Island at 10,000ft, the sweep leader ordered VF-15 to go down through the light overcast to reconnoiter Lahug airfield near the city while VF-19 remained as cover. The VF-15 pilots saw the airfield filled with single-engine airplanes and immediately went down to strafe the field, making three passes. Seeing no enemy aircraft airborne, VF-19 quickly dropped down to add to the destruction, setting fire to numerous single-engine fighters and twin-engine airplanes. VF-19's commander then saw fighters taking off from Opon airfield on Mactan Island, five miles away. He ordered VF-15 to cover Lahug while VF-19 went to take on the fighters over Opon, but the airfields were in such close proximity that the two squadrons found themselves fighting over both areas. VF-15 pilots considered 16 Hellcats barely adequate to take on the number of Japanese fighters in the air, particularly as in the initial fights many of the Japanese pilots were individually aggressive although very few fought as sections for mutual defense. In the intense fighting over Cebu city and the airfields, VF-15 claimed 17 Japanese fighters shot down with several more destroyed or damaged on the ground, but two Hellcat pilots were lost during the combat. VF-19 claimed 12 airplanes shot down and four more probables. The claims were mostly for Zekes and Oscars, but a few pilots made claims for Tojos (Ki-44) which may have been a case of misidentification.

Shortly after the start of the combat around Cebu, Task Group 38.1's fighter sweep arrived on the scene, with 12 Hellcats from VF-14 and 14 from VF-21, heading for Negros. The two squadrons found only a few aircraft, claiming four shot down and several damaged, but spotted a small convoy of seven freighters along the northeast coast of Cebu. VF-14's Hellcats each carried a single 500lb bomb, while seven of VF-21's airplanes were armed with 5" rockets. The Hellcats attacked the freighters with bombs and rockets and heavy strafing leaving several of the ships burning fiercely.

Three cargo ships burning in Cebu harbor. Japanese shipping was a priority target during the strikes on the Philippines. (80G-247511, RG80, NARA)

The first strike forces followed closely behind the fighter sweeps. Task Group 38.3 sent a large force of 82 aircraft, 34 from CVG-15, 36 from CVG-19, and 12 from CVLG-32, to bomb enemy shipping and harbor installations in Cebu and nearby Mactan Island. Flying escort to the bombers and torpedo bombers of VB-15 and VT-15, VF-15 arrived over the target area while the melee between the fighter sweep aircraft and Japanese fighters was still in progress. Flying cover above the bombers, VF-15 claimed a Dinah snooper while en route to the target area and nine single-engine fighters over Cebu and Mactan (seven Zekes and two Jacks, which again might be another case of misidentification). After their air combats, the Hellcats went down to bomb and strafe shipping in Cebu harbor. VB-15's Helldivers bombed the three main piers at Cebu and hit oil storage tanks on Mactan. The torpedo bombers went after Opon airfield on Mactan firing rockets and bombing airplanes in revetments and buildings on the airfield. One Avenger failed to return from the strike.

VF-19 sent 15 Hellcats to escort 15 VB-19 Helldivers, seven VT-19 Avengers, and four from VT-32 to bomb targets at Cebu. The fighters claimed only two Zekes shot down, but one of VB-19's SB2C-3s also claimed a Zeke after pulling out of a dive and beginning a strafing run on shipping in the harbor. Seeing a Zeke approaching his section, the pilot turned into the Zeke firing his 20mm wing cannon. As the Zeke turned away, the SB2C pilot turned with him, hitting the Zeke's engine and sending it down into the water four miles south of Cebu harbor. The rest of the bombers hit shipping in the harbor, claiming several large freighters sunk or left burning. VT-19 and VT-32 attacked Lahug, each TBM carrying a dozen 100lb bombs. The pilots estimated that upwards of 100 aircraft were on the field. The TBMs released their bombs on concentrations of aircraft, claiming 14 as probably destroyed.

The fighter sweep and the air combats during the first strike appear to have knocked out many of the Japanese fighters in the Cebu area. Task Group 38.3's subsequent second and third strikes encountered no Japanese aircraft. CVG-15 and CVG-19 combined in the second strike, with CVLG-32 joining CVG-15 for the third strike. On the second strike, VB-19 hit targets on the airfields and the harbor, claiming 20 single-engine and four twin-engine aircraft destroyed at one of the Cebu airfields, as well as hits on an oiler and freighter. VT-19

Planes from Air Group 14 begin an attack on a Japanese freighter. That day the Helldivers of VB-14 claimed serious damage to four cargo ships. (Air Group 14 Action Report for September 12, 1944, RG38, NARA)

bombed shipping, the Cebu dock area, and oil storage tanks, losing one TBM to antiaircraft fire. CVG-15 joined in attacking the harbor area and shipping in the second strike of the day, as well as hitting piers and the oil storage tanks. Combined attacks from fighters, dive bombers, and the torpedo bombers claimed to have sunk two medium-size freighters and damaged other ships. While CVG-19 attacked shipping north of Cebu, CVG-15 and CVLG-32 flew on to attack Dumaguete airfield at the southern tip of Negros. Encountering no opposition in the air, the squadrons found many single-engine aircraft on the airfield that they identified as Zekes and Oscars. In combined bombing and strafing attacks the two air groups believed they had destroyed, probably destroyed, or damaged an estimated 25 Japanese fighters.

Task Group 38.1's first strike following its fighter sweep was also against targets around Cebu town. The *Hornet*'s VF-2, escorting the strike force, ran into the Japanese fighters still fighting in the area, claiming nine Zekes and an Irving shot down over Mactan Island for the loss of one Hellcat. The fighters went on to strafe shipping in Cebu harbor. VB-2 attacked the airfield near the town and on Mactan Island, dropping 1,000lb bombs on aircraft parked on the fields. One division of Helldivers claimed 14 probably destroyed and eight damaged near Cebu while two other Helldivers claimed two probably destroyed and four damaged at Mactan. VT-2 added to the destruction on the airfield, bombing the runway and parked aircraft, with one Avenger setting fire to a twin-engine airplane in a strafing run.

CVG-14 joined in the attack on shipping in the harbor and on Mactan airfield. The Helldivers of VB-14 hit buildings, revetments, and antiaircraft positions at Mactan and then went after shipping, dropping 500lb bombs singly and strafing ships after pulling out of their dives. The Avengers of VT-14 dropped bombs on barracks buildings and revetments, then strafed the airfield before going on to attack shipping in the harbor. As one of the TBMs pulled up from a run on an oil tanker, the pilot found himself heading directly for a Pete floatplane fighter (Mitsubishi FM-1). He opened fire but missed. A second TBM, going in the same direction as the Pete, pulled up alongside so the Avenger's turret gunner could fire from a nearly perfect position. After only ten rounds the gunner's machine gun jammed. Several other Avengers strafed an Emily flying boat (Kawanishi H8K2) beached on a nearby island.

Task Group 38.1's second strike of the day targeted airfields on the island of Negros. Eight VF-2 Hellcats flew escort to ten SB2C-3s from VB-2, eight F6F-5 fighter bombers from VB-2, and six TBM-1Cs from VT-2. These attacked Manapla and Saravia airfields in the northwest of Negros. As the Avengers began their attack on Manapla airfield, between ten and 12 Zekes came in on the bombers but VF-2's Hellcats drove them off, claiming four Zekes shot down and three more as probables. In bombing attacks the Helldivers, Hellcat fighter bombers, and the Avengers claimed an estimated 15 aircraft destroyed and 25 more probably damaged.

CVG-14 also sent a force that hit the airfields on Negros, though initially assigned to attack shipping near Panay Island. Eight Hellcats from VF-14 escorted eight SB2C-3s and eight F6F-5 fighter bombers from VB-14 and eight TBM-1Cs from VT-14. When the force saw the target area covered in cloud, the planes headed to their secondary target, the airfields on Negros. The bombers attacked aircraft parked at what they believed to be Manapla airfield,

Airfields on Cebu and Negros were also targeted during the strikes on September 12. Air Group 15 attacked the airfield at Dumaguete on Negros, setting several Japanese aircraft on fire. (Air Group 15 Action Report for September 12, 1944, RG38, NARA)

seeing some 30 twin-engine and single-engine aircraft. The Helldivers and Avengers bombed and strafed parked aircraft and buildings on the airfield. VB-14's fighter bomber pilots turned in a remarkable performance. The Helldiver pilots chosen to fly the Hellcats as fighter bombers had not trained as fighter pilots and had only a hurried transition on to the Hellcat. As the CVG-14 formation came in to attack the airfield, with the fighter bombers leading the attack, they saw 20–30 Japanese aircraft in the air that they identified as Oscars (Ki-43), Nicks (Ki-45), and even some Nates (Ki-27). Coming off their strafing run on the field, the fighter bomber pilots immediately engaged the Japanese aircraft above them in their first experience of air combat. In a flurry of combats the fighter bomber pilots claimed five Oscars and three Nicks shot down, an Oscar probably shot down, and damage to a fourth Nick and two Nates, a highly credible performance. In the same action two of VB-14's rear gunners claimed Japanese aircraft shot down, a Nick and an Oscar. While withdrawing after the airfield attacks VF-14 engaged a group of capable Oscar pilots who, as stated in the Aircraft Action Report, "pressed home their attacks more vigorously than any this squadron has yet encountered." The Japanese pilots attacked from above, coming in out of the sun, trying to get in on the tails of the Hellcats then quickly climbing away. What saved the Hellcats was poor gunnery on the part of the Japanese pilots; not one Hellcat received any damage. The VF-14 pilots claimed six fighters destroyed and four damaged, including a Nick and a Nate. One VF-14 pilot submitted claims for two Hamps destroyed and two damaged, but these were almost certainly Oscars.

EVENTS

1. **0733–0740hrs.** Air Group 14 squadrons (VB-14, VF-14, and VT-14) take off from USS *Wasp* and proceed to Dumaguete airfield on Negros. VB-14 sends seven SB2C Helldivers and three F6F Hellcat fighter bombers, VF-14 sends 12 F6F Hellcats with three carrying 500lb bombs, and VT-14 sends seven TBM Avengers. VB-14 and VT-14 fly in separate formations with VF-14 providing close escort cover above.

2. **0915–0925hrs.** The formation approaches the airfield from the north, flying at 13,000ft. The squadrons pass the airfield then execute a 180° turn to attack from the southwest. The squadrons begin their attack from 11,000ft with one division of VF-14 remaining above as high cover.

3. **0930–0940hrs.** In a dive bombing attack, the SB2Cs release their bombs at 2,000ft. Employing glide bombing, the TBMs and the F6Fs release their bombs between 2,000ft and 3,500ft. The attacking aircraft hit buildings, parked aircraft, revetments, and the runway. One division of VF-14 F6Fs comes in to strafe the airfield.

4. **0940–0950hrs.** The squadrons pass over the airfield, dropping down to low altitude.

5. **0950–1015hrs.** The squadrons turn back to make repeated strafing passes across the airfield, leaving five airplanes in flames and others damaged.

6. **1015hrs.** The squadrons head for the rendezvous point over the sea to the east of the airfield. Hit by anti-aircraft fire, one VT-14 TBM makes a water landing. Two crewmen are rescued the next day.

7. **1158–1211hrs.** The squadrons return to the *Wasp*.

Air Group 14 attacks Dumaguete airfield on Negros, 13 September, 1944

The airfields on northern Negros were the main targets for the carrier air groups on September 13. Bacolod airfield came under attack from several air groups. (Air Group 14 Action Report for September 13, 1944, RG38, NARA)

Carrier Air Groups 2 and 14 attacked Bacolod after Carrier Air Group 15's first strike, adding to the destruction of aircraft and facilities around the field. (Air Group 14 Action Report for September 13, 1944, RG38, NARA)

By the end of the day on September 12, Task Force 38's squadrons had submitted claims for 82 Japanese aircraft destroyed in the air and 89 destroyed on the ground. VF-15 was the high scorer of the day, with claims for 27 Japanese aircraft shot down. Given the intensity of combat during the early morning fighter sweeps and strikes it is not surprising that claims exceeded probable losses. The 201st Naval Air Group lost at least 27 Zero fighters shot down, with 25 pilots killed, including a difficult-to-replace squadron leader. The 30th and 31st Air Regiments lost several aircraft in the air battles over Negros as did the 45th Air Regiment. Damage to shipping and port facilities was heavy. Postwar analysis confirmed that carrier aircraft sank an oil tanker and 11 freighters of different sizes around Cebu.

The next day, September 13, Task Force 38's three task groups concentrated on striking more airfields on northern Negros with several return strikes against the harbor installations and the Mactan airfield at Cebu town and attacks on Japanese shipping. The attacks began with fighter sweeps over Cebu and Negros, with the first strike following quickly behind. Between 0730hrs and 0830hrs the sweep and strike forces met over 100 Japanese aircraft in the air over northwest Negros, claiming 80 shot down.

Commander David McCampbell, CAG of CVG-15, led the first fighter sweep of 12 Hellcats from VF-15 and 12 from VF-19 from Task Group 38.3. After sweeping the Cebu area and encountering no opposition, McCampbell ordered VF-19 to break off and cover the incoming strike group from CVG-15 and CVG-19. Continuing on to Bacolod airfield on the northwest coast of Negros, the VF-15 fighters shot down two Betty bombers just taking off from the field before dropping down to strafe the field just before the first strike group arrived. Making repeated runs across the field, the Hellcats left 19 Japanese aircraft in flames before breaking off to cover the strike group. As the Hellcats climbed up to cover the bombers ten miles west of the airfield, one of the bombers called out Japanese aircraft coming in to attack. The VF-15 pilots saw many Oscar and Nate (Ki-27) fighters approaching and turned to intercept. The air battle lasted for the next 45 minutes against an estimated 35 to 45 Oscars and Nates that came in during the fighting. VF-15 claimed 22 Japanese aircraft shot down, including 13 Nates, for the loss of one Hellcat shot down. These aircraft were from the 32nd Flying Training Unit (32nd Kyōiku Hikotai) that were returning from a training flight when they ran into the Hellcats, losing 12 aircraft.

At the same time, seven VF-8 Hellcats off *Bunker Hill* joined fighters from VF-31 off the *Cabot* and VF-18 off the *Intrepid* to carry out fighter sweeps over Legaspi airfield on southern Luzon. On the first sweep, three VF-8 Hellcats joined two VF-31 divisions, arriving over Legaspi at 0745hrs. Seeing airplanes taking off below, the VF-31 pilot leading the sweep ordered the three VF-8 Hellcats to remain above as top cover, while he went down with his two divisions to attack. Engaging Japanese fighters they identified as

Tojos (Ki-44), the VF-31 pilots claimed three shot down with another probable, as well as a Zeke and a Tony destroyed. With no aircraft above, the three VF-8 pilots came down and engaged a Zeke, shooting it down. The *Cabot* and *Bunker Hill* fighters then made strafing runs over the airfield, VF-31 claiming two Bettys, a Jill, and a Judy destroyed, while the VF-8 division leader claimed three Bettys and a Zeke set on fire. Antiaircraft fire hit a VF-31 Hellcat, the pilot making a water landing off the coast. VF-8 lost a Hellcat to a Zero that hit the Hellcat's oil line, this pilot too making a water landing. OS2U Kingfishers from Task Force 38 cruisers rescued both pilots.

Task Groups 38.1 and 38.3 sent their first strikes against Bacolod airfield on Negros, while a smaller number of aircraft hit targets around Cebu town and nearby Mactan airfield. From TG38.1 CVG-2, CVG-14, and CVLG-22 sent out 79 fighters, dive bombers, and torpedo bombers, while TG38.3 sent 72 aircraft from CVG-15, CVG-19, and CVLG-27. CVG-2 and CVG-14 were scheduled to attack shipping off Panay Island, north of Negros, but when the strike force saw the target area covered in cloud the force turned to attack Bacolod airfield. Coming in toward Bacolod at 9,000ft, the SB2C-3 pilots of VB-2 saw columns of smoke rising from the airfield from VF-15's previous strafing attack. The Helldivers went into their dives, dropping 1,000lb bombs on the field and strafing with 20mm cannon. Four of VB-2's F6F-5 Hellcat fighter bombers dropped 500lb bombs on the field and went down to strafe, the formation claiming six aircraft destroyed in their attack. One of the Hellcat pilots claimed a Zeke shot down after pulling out of his strafing run. VF-2 Hellcats escorting the bombers claimed three Nates and two Zekes attempting to intercept the bombers. CVG-14 added to the destruction, bombing buildings on the field and the runway, but found no other good targets. Eleven Hellcats from VF-22 strafed and rocketed the field, hitting several buildings. Returning from the attack VF-22 pilots came across two Dinah reconnaissance aircraft (Ki-46) and shot them down.

While CVG-19 and CVLG-27 hit targets at Cebu town and nearby Mactan airfield, CVG-15 joined in the attack on Bacolod airfield on Negros. With seven VF-15 Hellcats as escort, VB-15 and VT-15 came in over Bacolod at 10,000ft. The Helldivers dropped their bombs on parked aircraft while the Avengers used glide bombing attacks against hangars and revetment areas. The VF-15 Hellcats went down to strafe and fire rockets at parked aircraft, claiming three medium bombers destroyed. As the strike formation flew past the northwestern tip of Negros, some 20 to 25 Oscars and Zekes attacked, but the VF-15 pilots broke up the attacks and claimed eight Japanese fighters destroyed. The fighters gave credit to the bombers who flew in tight formation, shepherding a damaged F6F from another squadron in their midst, while the gunners kept up a stream of fire at any approaching Japanese fighter.

At the same time that Task Groups 38.1 and 38.3 were attacking Bacolod, Task Group 38.2 sent its first strike force composed of aircraft from CVG-8 and CVLG-31 to attack Fabrica airfield on the northeast coast of Negros. As the strike force approached Fabrica, they saw 30 to 40 Japanese fighters which they identified as 10 to 15 Zekes and 15 to 20 Oscars. They were all more likely to have been Oscars from the 30th and 31st Fighter Regiments that took off to intercept the strike force. Escorting the Helldivers and Avengers

Saravia airfield, one of several airfields at the northern end of Negros Island, also came under attack that day. The proximity of these airfields and a lack of good photographic coverage before the carrier strikes, led to some confusion as to which airfield the air groups actually struck. (Task Group 38.1 Action Report for September 12, 1944, RG38, NARA)

A sunken cargo ship can be seen in the water just off the wing tip of a Helldiver taking photographs of the destruction on September 14. Burning oil tanks hit earlier send up oily black smoke. (80G-247513, RG80, NARA)

of VB-8 and VT-8, the Hellcats of VF-8 took on the Oscars, not one of which managed to reach the bombers. Despite the fact that VF-8 lost two Hellcats shot down, the VF-8 pilots thought that the Japanese pilots were inferior and not as aggressive as the Japanese fighters they had engaged over the Marianas in June. VF-8 claimed 11 fighters shot down with two probables and four damaged over the airfield. Not to be outdone, several of the Helldivers fired on Japanese fighters as the SB2Cs pulled out of their dives, claiming one (identified as a Hamp) shot down.

Escorting four TBMs from VT-22 and bombers from CVG-8, with a division to the right of the formation and a second division on the left, VF-31 also engaged the Oscars. When some of the Japanese fighters were reported coming in from astern, the VF-31 pilots did a 180 degree turn to face them head on, firing to drive the Oscars away from the bombers and diving after the Japanese fighters as they spiraled away from the bombers. The combat continued as the bombers attacked the airfield. VB-8's Helldivers claimed a Betty bomber and a Zeke left burning and five to seven more aircraft damaged, while in glide bombing attacks VT-8 and VT-31 dropped 500lb bombs on parked aircraft in revetment areas, claiming two more Betty bombers and 13 other aircraft destroyed. VF-31's pilots claimed 19 Oscars and a single Tony destroyed, one Oscar probably destroyed, and six damaged for the loss of one pilot who ran out of fuel and was killed making a water landing near the Task Force.

CVG-18 accompanied CVG-8 and CVLG-31 to Negros, but went on to attack Bacolod and Alicante airfields, and possibly the airfields at Silay and Cadiz. The air groups did not have good Intelligence about the airfields and as they were near each other it was sometimes difficult to determine which airfield was attacked. Seven of VB-18's SB2C-3s bombed Silay airfield, cratering the runway, but five flew on to Cadiz airfield in search of better targets. Here the bombers found 20 to 25 aircraft parked around the airfield. They destroyed two aircraft with bombs and another two in strafing attacks, damaging five to seven more. VT-18's Avengers made a glide bombing attack on what they thought was Bacolod, and then another attack on nearby Alicante airfield dropping down to strafe the airfield. One TBM pilot violated standing orders not to strafe below 1,500ft, coming in at 300ft where antiaircraft fire shot down his aircraft. VF-18's Hellcats also engaged the attacking Oscars, claiming eight destroyed (identifying these as Hamps and Zekes as well as Oscars), but losing one Hellcat to antiaircraft fire on a strafing run over Manapla airfield west of Fabrica.

The attacks on the airfields on Negros continued during the day, but there were no more encounters with groups of Japanese fighter aircraft. In the morning combats the 30th and 31st Fighter Regiments lost 16 to 20 Ki-43s while claiming six to ten American aircraft. For its second strike of the morning Task Group 38.1 sent CVG-2, CVG-14, and CVLG-22 to bomb Dumaguete airfield at the southern end of Negros. There were 10 to 15 single-engine aircraft on the field. The bombers hit the runway, revetment areas, and buildings on the airfield and claimed damage to several aircraft. Antiaircraft fire hit a VT-14 TBM which had to make a water landing east of Negros. SOC and OS2U aircraft rescued two of the crew the next day. Task Group 38.2 sent CVG-8, CVG-14, and CVLG-31 to hit the airfield at Tacloban on Leyte and the airfields and shipping around Cebu. All three task groups sent aircraft back to the Negros airfields for their third strike. CVG-19 and CVLG-27 claimed 15 aircraft destroyed on the ground at Saravia airfield on Negros. By the afternoon there were so few worthwhile targets remaining that Task Group 38.1 and Task Group 38.3 sent their last strike of the day to bomb harbor installations and shipping at Cebu, leaving Task Group 38.2 to make one last strike against the airfields on Negros, switching to hitting Medallin airfield on Cebu when cloud covered the Negros airfields.

The damage inflicted during the day was even greater than the day before. The air groups submitted claims for 94 Japanese aircraft shot down over the Visayas or approaching the Task Force, with ten probably destroyed and an additional 20 damaged. Aircraft claimed destroyed on the ground amounted to 105 single- and twin-engine aircraft, with most of the destruction on Bacolod and Fabrica airfields. While none of the airfields were put out of action, the damage to installations was considerable. In addition, the air groups continued their attacks on Japanese shipping around the Visayas, claiming several ships sunk or damaged.

A TBM-1C from VT-31 takes the barrier on USS *Cabot* during the September strikes on the Visayas. Operational losses were a constant feature of carrier operations. (80G-268113, RG80, NARA)

Like the day before, the Japanese response to the carrier strikes was almost negligible. At dawn the Task Force began picking up bogies on radar. At 0555hrs the *Lexington* spotted a Japanese airplane tentatively identified as a Judy making a bombing and strafing run against the carrier. A large bomb fell some 30yds astern. The *Lexington* opened fire with its 20mm and 40mm guns, but failed to hit the Judy which continued on through the task group. Another bogey appeared on radar at 0600hrs. A CAP from VF-21 off the *Belleau Wood* intercepted and shot down a Frances. Shortly after launching the first strike of the day, a lone Oscar appeared over Task Group 38.3 diving on the *Langley*, dropping a bomb which fell several hundred yards astern. The *Essex*, *Princeton*, and ships in the task group's screen opened fire, shooting down the Oscar. A short time later the VF-21 CAP claimed another Oscar shot down near the Task Force. It is likely that all the aircraft which attempted to bomb the carriers were from a flight of four Ki-43s from the 30th Fighter Regiment sent out to attack the American Task Force. Only one pilot returned, Lt Fujimoto Katsumi claiming to have hit an American cruiser.

F6F Hellcat versus Ki-45 Nick over Negros

On September 12, 1944, Task Force 38 launched strikes against targets on Cebu and Negros in the Visayas. Among the targets that day were airfields on northern Negros. VB-14, flying off USS *Wasp* (CV-18), was tasked with attacking the airfield at Manapla. A few weeks before the September strikes VB-14 exchanged ten of its SB2C-3 Helldivers for ten F6F-3/5 Hellcats to evaluate the effectiveness of using the Hellcat as a fighter bomber in place of the Helldiver. Sixteen pilots received an hour of flying time in the Hellcat and, en route to Palau and the Philippines, practiced glide bombing. Though experienced, none of the pilots assigned to fly the Hellcats had ever engaged in aerial combat. In the attack on Manapla airfield, VB-14 encountered Ki-43 Oscar and Ki-45 Nick twin-engine fighters. In the ensuing combat, VB-14's Hellcat pilots acquitted themselves with distinction, claiming five Oscars and three Nicks shot down. Lt Allen Lewis and Lt S.T. Elway both claimed an Oscar and a Nick destroyed. This combat proved the flexibility of the Hellcat as a fighter bomber and a fighter, adding to the offensive and defensive power of fighter sweeps.

That evening Admiral Halsey submitted a bold recommendation to Admiral Nimitz. The weak Japanese response to the attacks on the Visaya airfields, the damage his carrier aircraft had inflicted on Japanese Army and Navy aircraft, and the failure to strike at his Task Force convinced Halsey that the central Philippines were "a hollow shell with weak defenses and skimpy facilities." Aware that the Combined Chiefs of Staff were anxious to speed victory in the Pacific, Halsey proposed skipping the planned capture of the Palaus, Yap, the Talaud Islands, and Mindanao, and advancing the date for the invasion of Leyte. Still unaware that the Japanese were holding back their forces waiting for the decisive battle, Halsey wrote Nimitz that "the enemy's non-aggressive attitude was unbelievable and fantastic." Halsey believed the central Philippines was wide open. Nimitz however was unwilling to cancel the capture of Palau, which he believed important to securing MacArthur's right flank, but he forwarded Halsey's recommendation on to the Joint Chiefs of Staff, who were meeting their British counterparts at the OCTAGON Conference in Quebec. Nimitz contacted MacArthur offering him the forces freed up from cancelling the Yap and Mindanao operations. MacArthur's Chief of Staff agreed that the intermediate operations could be cancelled and the attack on Leyte advanced to October 20 from December 20.

The Joint Chiefs were having dinner with their Canadian hosts when Halsey's recommendations and MacArthur's concurrence arrived. Admiral Leahy, President Roosevelt's Chief of Staff, Admiral King, General Marshall, and General Arnold quickly excused themselves and deliberated on the recommendations from the Pacific. As Marshall later wrote, "Having the utmost confidence in General MacArthur, Admiral Nimitz, and Admiral Halsey, it was not a difficult decision to make." Ninety minutes after receiving the recommendation the Joint Chiefs sent instructions to Nimitz and MacArthur to cancel the Yap, Talaud Islands, and Mindanao operations and advance the date for the invasion of Leyte to October 20. This was, without doubt, the most important outcome of the September strikes against the Philippines.

September 14 was the last day of strikes against the Visayas. Task Group 38.1 had departed the previous evening for Morotai to support the landings scheduled for September 15. Task Groups 38.2 and 38.3 remained off the Visayas to make the final strikes against the airfields on Negros. The objective of these missions was to destroy any remaining Japanese aircraft on the airfields. Operations began with fighter sweeps ahead of the first strikes on the airfields. Task Group 38.2's CVG-8 sent 11 Hellcats from VF-8 on a sweep over the airfields on northern Negros with 16 Hellcats from VF-18 flying as top cover. After searching for a reported convoy off the northern tip of Cebu, the fighters did not encounter any Japanese aircraft in the air so the divisions separated to seek targets of opportunity. The VF-8 Hellcats went down to strafe what they identified as Lanog-lanog airfield, another name for Alicante airfield. The pilots strafed aircraft around the airfield, reporting hits on Bettys, Topsy transports, and Zeke and Oscar fighters, all of which appeared to have been previously damaged, as only one Betty bomber started smoking. The Hellcats from VF-18 were also confused as to which airfields they attacked, believing they hit Manapla and Cadiz on the northern tip of Negros. The pilots claimed a Zeke, three Oscars, and a twin-engine aircraft as probably destroyed after multiple passes across the airfields. At the same time, CVLG-31 sent eight VF-31 Hellcats on a sweep over Legaspi airfield where they found no aircraft but knocked out a steam engine.

Task Group 38.3's fighter sweeps had a more productive morning. The *Essex* and *Lexington* sent off ten Hellcats from VF-15 and 12 from VF-19 on a sweep over central Panay Island and the Negros airfields. VF-15 found no aircraft airborne over central Panay, but did strafe aircraft on the ground at Santa Barbara airfield, ten miles north of Iloilo town, claiming nine aircraft destroyed. The squadron then flew to Saravia airfield on Negros where the pilots claimed seven more aircraft destroyed, and one aircraft destroyed on Fabrica. VF-19 also flew to Panay, claiming three aircraft destroyed on the ground at an airfield near Iloilo.

Returning to northern Negros, VF-19's Hellcats strafed Manapla and Fabrica airfields where they made repeated runs across the airfields, claiming 13 airplanes destroyed, 12 probably destroyed, and a further 26 damaged.

The two task groups sent out several strikes to the Visayas to inflict more damage on aircraft hit during the previous two days of strikes. Task Group 38.2's air groups made two strikes against the airfields on northern Negros. CVG-8 hit Saravia on the first strike, and returned to Bacolod on the second, while CVG-18 struck Manapla first, then Alicante on the second strike of the day. VB-8 and VT-8 bombed buildings and claimed one aircraft destroyed at Saravia, and a few damaged at Bacolod, returning with a report of few worthwhile targets left at either field. At Manapla CVG-18's squadrons claimed only one aircraft destroyed and three Oscars probably damaged, but three aircraft destroyed, three probably destroyed, and four more damaged during the second strike on Alicante.

Pilots of VF-18 on board USS *Intrepid* (CV-11) gather at the tail of an F6F-3 following a mission. Ruggedly built, straightforward to fly and land on a carrier, the F6F equipped all the fighter squadrons in the Fast Carrier Task Force in September 1944. (National Museum of Naval Aviation)

Task Group 38.3's air groups made their first strike against Panay, with CVG-15 hitting buildings and installations at Santa Barbara airfield while CVG-19 and CVLG-32 bombed targets at Iloilo. Returning from this strike two VF-32 pilots claimed an Oscar and a Zero destroyed at Saravia. On the second strike, to Manapla and Fabrica, CVG-19 hit buildings on the airfields and claimed five aircraft destroyed. CVG-15 found no suitable targets so went on to bomb installations around the Iloilo harbor. CVG-19 returned to La Carlotta airfield on Negros, accompanied by CVLG-32, for the last strike on the airfields. At La Carlotta CVG-19 hit more buildings on the field and left five aircraft burning. VF-32 claimed seven aircraft destroyed at La Carlotta from strafing, and nine more aircraft destroyed on the ground at a second airfield nearby.

While en route to Morotai, on September 14, Task Group 38.1 sent off a strike against airfields around Davao on Mindanao, finding the area devoid of Japanese aircraft. The strike aircraft hit buildings on the airfields, but sank the 1,500 ton Japanese Navy High Speed Transport HO5 off Davao. At the same time, the *Cowpens* and *Belleau Wood* launched 16 Hellcats from VF-21 and 16 from VF-22 on a long-range strike against the Japanese airfield at Zamboanga on the southwestern tip of Mindanao. The airfield was nearly 350 miles from the task group, the pilots spending 4 hours and 37 minutes in the air. They were rewarded for their effort, finding 16 twin-engine and five single-engine aircraft at the airfield. Using rockets and their .50 caliber machine guns, the VF-21 and VF-22 pilots claimed six Betty bombers, a Nick twin-engine fighter, and two single-engine aircraft destroyed, with five more Bettys and three twin-engine aircraft probably destroyed. Seeing three freighters in Zamboanga harbor, two VF-22 divisions attacked these ships with rockets and strafing, damaging all three.

The three days of strikes against the Visayas had been far more productive than the earlier strikes against Mindanao. Admiral Halsey was well pleased with the destruction his three task groups had wrought against Japanese air power in the central Philippines. Over the three days, Task Force 38's air groups had flown 2,057 sorties claiming 168 Japanese aircraft shot down over the Visayas and an additional five shot down on search missions or over the Task Force. The attacks on shipping resulted in claims for six Japanese Navy ships sunk and 31 merchant ships of various sizes. The strikes had hit installations at all the airfields attacked and badly damaged buildings and facilities at Cebu and Iloilo harbors. The cost to Task Force 38 was less than expected. Japanese aircraft and antiaircraft fire shot down ten Hellcat fighters and two Hellcat fighter bombers, four Helldivers, and six Avengers, with the loss of 12 pilots and 14 aircrew. SOC and OS2U floatplanes from the task groups had successfully rescued several flyers off the Visayas. At the conclusion of the Visaya strikes Halsey sent a signal to his carriers: "Because of the brilliant performance my group of stars has just given, I am booking you to appear before the best audience in the Asiatic theater." The success of the strikes on the Visayas and the weak Japanese opposition emboldened Halsey to strike at Manila, the heart of the Philippines, and the center of Japanese air power and shipping. When he sensed a weakness in his enemy, he was determined to exploit it.

The strikes on Luzon, September 21–22, 1944

Following the successful strikes on the Visayas, Task Groups 38.2 and 38.3 retired to a designated fuel rendezvous south of Palau, where the carriers took on fuel oil and aviation gasoline and received replacement aircraft and pilots from the escort carrier USS *Barnes* (CVE-20). On September 17, Task Group 38.2 flew missions in support of the landings on Peleliu and Angaur, while Task Group 38.3 was on standby. The day after, Task Group 38.4 was relieved of duty supporting the Palau invasion and retired to the anchorage at Manus in the Admiralties for replenishment. Task Group 38.1 now rejoined Task Force 38 having covered the landings at Morotai on September 15–16.

The Navy's Seventh Fleet provided direct air support for the Morotai invasion. Task Group 38.1 acted as a covering force, available to supplement the Seventh Fleet escort carriers if necessary and to prevent any intervention by the Japanese Navy. On the way to Morotai the task group sent out several long-range search missions of SB2C aircraft looking for enemy activity in the islands north of the Celebes and in the northeastern Celebes. On September 15, the day of the landings on Morotai, Task Group 38.1 maintained combat air patrols over Morotai, VF-2 claiming one Betty bomber shot down while on CAP duty. That same morning the task group sent off an early fighter sweep against the Japanese airfield at Langoan, near the town of Manado in the northeastern tip of the Celebes with 14 Hellcats from VF-21 off *Belleau Wood* and 16 from VF-22 off *Cowpens*. The Hellcats each carried six

Primary objectives for the strikes on Luzon were, as with the strikes on the Visayas, Japanese air power and shipping. Smoke billows up from Nichols Field, near Manila, under attack on the morning of September 21, 1944. The photo was taken by an airplane from Air Group 15. (80G-46794, RG80, NARA)

5" HVAR rockets. The squadrons found a large number of aircraft on the ground at Langoan and in repeated strafing runs using rockets and machine guns, claimed 28 single- and twin-engine Japanese aircraft destroyed.

With no Japanese aircraft opposing the Morotai invasion, and no evidence of Japanese naval vessels in the area, Task Group 38.1 completed its assignment on the afternoon of September 16 and headed to Palau to rejoin Task Force 38. On arrival in the area on September 18, the *Belleau Wood* was relieved of duty with Task Group 38.1 and transferred to Task Group 38.4, with USS *Monterey* and CVLG-28 joining Task Group 38.1 as a replacement. The task groups completed refueling and receiving replacement aircraft and pilots then, on September 20, sortied northwest for the Philippines. By midnight the three task groups had reached a position 300 miles east of Manila. They then began a high-speed run to bring the carriers to within 70 miles of the central coast of Luzon by dawn under cover of a weather front.

Attacking Luzon had not been part of Admiral Halsey's original operational plan for strikes on the Philippines. The weak Japanese response to the attacks on Mindanao on September 9–10, however, persuaded Halsey to adopt a more aggressive plan. Attacking the base of such a large concentration of land-based air power was a definite risk. Allied Intelligence estimated that the Japanese Army and Navy had 531 aircraft based on Luzon, including 300 single- and twin-engine bombers with the range to reach Task Force 38 cruising off the Philippines. But the potential rewards were deemed greater than the potential risks. Luzon was a vital Japanese base. Manila and nearby Subic Bay were important shipping areas, with good anchorages and extensive docks and harbor facilities. The airfields around the old Clark Field, 30 miles north of Manila, and Nielson and Nichols Fields nearer the city, were extensive operational bases for the defense of the Philippines presenting an opportunity for inflicting maximum attrition on Japanese air power, as Admiral Nimitz wanted. These bases were also a key area for training Army and Navy pilots. With Japan increasingly short of experienced pilots, any disruption to the training effort would be an added bonus.

Task Force 38 assigned each task group to a specific set of targets. Task Group 38.1 was given the task of attacking Japanese shipping in Manila and southern Luzon over the two days of planned strikes. Task Group 38.2 was assigned to the complex of airfields around Clark Field, with half of its effort also devoted to shipping targets. Task Group 38.3 took on responsibility for attacking Nielson and Nichols Fields, and other fields around Manila and southern Luzon. This allocation allowed the air groups in each task group to become familiar with their targets and quickly disseminate tactical information while simplifying bomb loading.

More smoke and flames rise from Nichols Field as the strike aircraft hit more Japanese aircraft and installations around the field. (80G-281095, RG80, NARA)

Nearby Nielson Field came under attack at the same time as the attacks on Nichols Field. In this photo, bombs are exploding on installations and aircraft around the airfield. (80G-281080, RG80, NARA)

Opposing the carrier strikes were the Japanese Army's Ki-61 Tony fighters of the 17th Fighter Regiment, based at Angeles South near Clark Field, and the 19th Fighter Regiment based at Angeles West, with the Ki-43 Oscars of the 31st Fighter Regiment also based there. The Imperial Navy's 201st Air Group had Zero fighters based around Clark Field and at Nichols Field. Japanese radar picked up the approaching American strike forces, but once again there were problems getting a warning to the fighter units. The attacks on the morning of September 21 came as a surprise. When the Army and Navy fighters took off to intercept, the American aircraft were already attacking their targets.

The weather that provided cover for Task Force 38 on its approach to the Philippines delayed launching the preparatory fighter sweep for two hours. At around 0800hrs, 96 Hellcats from the air groups on board the light fleet carriers took off. VF-31 off the *Cabot* and VF(N)-41 off *Independence*, flying a mix of regular F6F Hellcats and Hellcat night fighters, were to attack Clark Field while VF-27 off *Princeton* and VF-32 off *Langley* covered Nichols and Nielson Fields. Task Group 38.1's CVLG fighter squadrons provided high cover for the sweep, with the newly arrived VF-28 off *Monterey* covering Task Group 38.2's squadrons and VF-22 off *Cowpens* covering Task Group 38.3.

In the poor weather after launching, VF(N)-41 could not join up with VF-31, so proceeded independently to Clark Field. The 16 Hellcats VF(N)-41 sent on the sweep comprised two F6F-3s, 12 F6F-5s (three of which were F6F-5Ns with their radar removed for this operations), and two F6F-5N night fighters, each Hellcat carrying a single 500lb bomb. Arriving in the area, the Hellcats proceeded to attack Clark Field by divisions, dropping their bombs on parked aircraft and nearby buildings, claiming several aircraft destroyed. Climbing back up to the rendezvous point VF(N)-41 ran into several Japanese aircraft that seemed to be unaware of the attack. For many of the pilots this was their first encounter with enemy aircraft. The Hellcat pilots claimed a Tony and a Topsy transport destroyed, with two more damaged, and a Zeke and an Oscar probably destroyed before heading back to their carrier.

VF-31 arrived over Clark Field as VF(N)-41 was completing its attack, the Hellcats remaining at altitude until VF(N)-41 left the area. Ten VF-31 Hellcats then went down to bomb and strafe the field, hitting parked aircraft and buildings though smoke and haze prevented a good look at the damage done. One Hellcat may have been damaged by antiaircraft fire as other pilots reported the aircraft struggling to gain altitude and the pilot never returned. By now the Japanese were responding to the attacks and someone soon tallyhoed bogies. Six of the Hellcats jettisoned their bombs and remained as cover for those bombing and strafing below. A melee erupted over the field, with the VF-31 pilots reporting fights with a mix of Tonys, Oscars, Zekes, and Tojos (possibly a misidentification as it is unclear if any Ki-44s were in fact stationed around Clark Field in September 1944). The pilots claimed six fighters shot down with two more probables and eight damaged. It appears that warnings of the attack had not spread to other aircraft, as VF-31 also claimed two Val dive bombers (D3A Type 99), a Nell bomber (G3M), an Emily four-engine flying boat (H8K2), and seven Topsy transports (Ki-57 or L4M) flying around the area.

An F6F-3 from VF-8 on a sweep around Subic Bay. CVG-8 carried out a strike on a convoy northwest of Subic Bay. On the return, VF-8 claimed 13 Japanese fighters shot down and a further three destroyed on the ground at San Marcelino Field. (80G-46787, RG80, NARA)

TBM Avengers from VT-28 off USS *Monterey* (CVL-26) approach Manila Bay. Four VT-28 Avengers joined VT-2 and VT-14 in attacks on Japanese shipping. (80G-281090, RG80, NARA)

VF-27 led the fighter sweep to Nielson and Nichols Fields with VF-32. Nichols Field was VF-27's assigned target. Four divisions made several strafing attacks against parked airplanes on the field, claiming at least eight destroyed, three probably destroyed, and four damaged. Two Hellcats destroyed an Emily flying boat moored at the former US Navy base at Cavite southwest of Manila and shot down a Nick flying nearby. As the pilots regained altitude they saw a large group of 30 to 40 Japanese fighters over Manila Bay, identifying these as a mix of Zekes, Hamps, Oscars, and Tonys. In the dogfight that followed, VF-27 claimed three Hamps, nine Zekes, one Oscar, and 17 Tonys shot down. The Japanese fighters damaged a few Hellcats, but VF-27 suffered no losses in the combat. The Hellcat pilots found that although they had a speed advantage, all the Japanese fighters could out-climb and out-maneuver the Hellcat at low altitude. The Tony pilots in particular appeared to have a good knowledge of tactics, bracketing the Hellcats and pressing home their attacks, the Hellcats countering with effective weaving and teamwork. As the squadron made its way to a rendezvous over Laguna de Bay, a large lake east of Manila, a group of 16 to 20 Tonys attacked the formation, losing seven to the Hellcats. This gave VF-27 a total of 38 claims for the day, the highest one day score of any of the fighter squadrons involved in the September carrier strikes.

VF-32 sent two divisions to reconnoiter Polillo Island east of Luzon, with four divisions continuing on to Manila to attack Nielson Field. The divisions orbited the field to search for enemy aircraft but on finding none went down to strafe parked aircraft on Nielson and on

The attack on Clark Field

Clark Field, north of Manila, was the center of Japanese Army and Navy aviation in the Philippines. After conquering the Philippines, the Japanese greatly expanded the runways and facilities at Clark Field and added half a dozen new airfields in the area. The Clark Field complex was a priority target for Task Force 38's strikes on Luzon. The first attack on Clark Field took place on September 21, 1944. VB-8, flying off USS *Bunker Hill* (CV-17), was the first squadron to attack. Lt Cdr J.D. Arbes led five Helldivers in a low-level attack on the field, dropping 100lb and 1,000lb bombs on buildings and parked aircraft, and strafing with the Helldiver's 20mm cannon while the rear gunners opened fire with their .30 caliber machine guns. The attack left five aircraft burning and seven or eight more damaged.

several smaller airfields in the area. The two divisions sent to Polillo rejoined the squadron over Manila and attacked the airfields. In total, VF-32 claimed 21 aircraft destroyed on the ground, including 14 Betty bombers left in flames, with 11 more aircraft damaged, but losing two Hellcats to intense antiaircraft fire. The divisions ran into several Japanese fighters in the air, shooting down three Tonys as they attempted to take off from an airfield near Nielson, and claiming two more plus two Zekes and a Hamp. One Hellcat had to make a water landing near the Task Force after suffering damage in combat with a Zero.

Task Group 38.1 carried out four strikes against shipping in Manila Bay with the *Hornet*'s CVG-2 and *Wasp*'s CVG-14 conducting the first three strikes, joined by four TBM-1C Avengers from VT-28 on the first strike of the day and four from VT-22 for the last strike. On the first strike CVG-2 sent out 12 VB-2 SB2C-3s and eight TBM-1Cs from VT-2. The strike force approached Manila Bay from the north, coming in at 10,000ft. VB-2 went after a group of ten freighters within the breakwater near the city, pushing over from 10,000ft, releasing the bombs at 3,000ft and pulling out at 1,000ft. Heavy antiaircraft fire from shore emplacements and the ships in the harbor interfered with the dives. The Helldivers had near misses on five freighters, but got three hits on a large tanker with 1,000lb bombs which exploded and sank.

VT-2 made its approach right after the SB2Cs completed their attack, circling to the west of Manila Bay then turning east for their attack. The torpedo pilots saw what they estimated to be 50 worthwhile shipping targets in the bay and behind the breakwater, although none of the larger warships that had been expected. The pilots later agreed that this was the most successful attack they had made in six months of combat. The Avengers made their run at 300–500ft, dropping their torpedoes 1,500–1,000yds from their targets. One torpedo malfunctioned, but seven ran "straight, hot, and true." One torpedo hit a large tanker which was seen to break apart and sink. Two pilots targeted a second tanker, which was also claimed as sunk, while the remaining two pilots launched their torpedoes against medium-size freighters, setting one on fire. VF-2 escorted the bombers to the target area, but at first seeing no enemy aircraft went down to strafe small vessels in the bay. While they were strafing, a formation of Tonys jumped the Hellcats for VF-2's first encounter with the Ki-61 fighter. The Hellcat pilots found that they could follow a Tony in a turn, and with War Emergency Power could out-climb the Japanese fighter. The Tony pilots were thought to be above average in flying skill but appeared to lack aggressiveness, failing to attack the bombers when they had the opportunity. In the fights over the bay and to the east, VF-2 claimed nine Tonys shot down, four probables, one damaged, and a Zeke shot down as well.

Japanese ships burning near Manila harbor after one of the shipping strikes. Task Force 38 carried out four strikes on shipping on September 21. The air groups claimed 55 small and large freighters and naval vessels sunk or probably sunk during the two days of strikes on Manila Bay. (80G-46792, RG80, NARA)

CVG-14's VT-14 also had an excellent mission, its first mass torpedo attack of the war. The squadron's ten Avengers circled while VB-14 carried out attacks on the ships in the bay, coming in from the northwest to attack a northern group of freighters anchored outside the breakwater. The dive bombers drew off the heavy flak while light and medium antiaircraft fire from the ships was inaccurate. The drops were successful, all ten torpedoes running straight to their targets achieving eight hits. Three pilots launched their torpedoes against the same large oil tanker, claiming three hits while three pairs of pilots attacked three medium-size freighters, sinking two and seriously damaging the third. A single torpedo pilot launched his torpedo against another freighter, claiming this as sunk. VB-2 attacked a floating drydock, several freighters, and claimed to have sunk a Japanese Navy destroyer, which may have been the *Satsuki*, just arrived in Manila after escorting a convoy from Singapore. This may also have been the Imperial Navy repair ship *Sunosaki*, which was also sunk that day in Manila Bay. Retirement was made to the west, but a Tony jumped one of the SB2Cs that was intent on strafing a ship and shot it down.

This first attack set the pattern for the subsequent strikes on shipping in Manila Bay. On the second and third strikes there were plenty of targets to choose from. With the plethora of targets, identifying which pilot hit which ship became the problem. VT-2 and VT-14 used torpedoes on their second strike, then switched to a load of four 500lb bombs for their third and fourth strikes. The SB2Cs added two 250lb bombs under their wings along with the standard 1,000lb bomb in the Helldiver's bomb bay. By the fourth strike in the afternoon the ships in Manila Bay had been heavily worked over. Some had gotten underway in an effort to escape the onslaught of bombing. In the smoke and haze it was difficult for pilots to distinguish an undamaged ship from a damaged one. Despite this, VB-14 had one of its most effective missions getting a high percentage of hits on five freighters and two oil tankers and starting 11 new fires. By the end of the day CVG-2 claimed to have sunk a destroyer type, three tankers, and three freighters, probably sunk six more, and damaged 12, while CVG-14 also put in a claim for a destroyer type, three tankers, and nine freighters sunk, as well as 13 ships damaged. The losses were surprisingly low, VT-2 losing one TBM-1C to antiaircraft fire on the fourth strike of the day, and VB-14 losing one SB2C-3 to the Tony and a second to antiaircraft fire.

An SB2C-3 from VB-2 pulls up and away after dive bombing shipping in Manila Bay. Near misses surround several freighters after the attack. (80G-342915, RG80, NARA)

Both VB-2 and VB-14 employed their Hellcat fighter bombers on two of their four shipping strikes. On VB-2's second strike the fighter bombers dived ahead of the Helldivers, getting several near misses on a destroyer type and then strafing several freighters. The fighter bombers proved their worth, and their versatility on the withdrawal from Manila. To the annoyance of some of the VB-2 pilots, their fighter compatriots could not resist the temptation to go down and strafe any ships they saw, leaving the bombers uncovered. As the bombers saw enemy aircraft during the rendezvous, they were grateful for the Hellcat fighter bombers that did provide cover for them. During the last strike of the day, four VB-2 fighter bombers attacked a medium size freighter with 500lb bombs, getting one direct hit and setting the ship on fire. After pulling out of their dives the four strafed a small tanker which exploded in flames. VB-14's fighter bombers participated in the first strike, with three Hellcats bombing and strafing a large freighter and one bombing a ship tied to a dock starting a large fire. On the third strike, the fighter bombers inflicted serious damage to four freighters with 500lb bombs and strafing. On retirement two of the Hellcats fought off two Tonys claiming damage to both, while a third damaged another Tony that had jumped him.

On this day Task Group 38.2 made two strikes against Clark Field, and two against shipping on the coast of Luzon west of Manila. Cloud cover frustrated the first strike on Clark Field. The weather delays over Task Force 38 resulted in CVG-8 and CVG-18 arriving over Clark Field before the fighter sweep. There was an overcast above the field and clouds below

OPPOSITE AIRFIELDS AROUND MANILA: KEY TARGETS FOR THE SEPTEMBER 21–22 STRIKES

obscuring the target area and making observation of bombing results difficult. VB-8's SB2C-1Cs led the attack, achieving complete surprise. The bombers encountered no antiaircraft fire on their first runs across the field, bombing first and returning to strafe with their 20mm cannons. The Avengers carried a load of 100lb general purpose and incendiary bombs, while the SB2Cs carried the usual 1,000lb bomb and two 100lb bombs under the wings. The bombers targeted buildings and hangars around the field and in between Clark North and Clark South runways, hitting parked aircraft where they could be seen. One Zeke and a Sally (Ki-21) bomber were taking off as the attack began. A gunner on a VB-8 SB2C shot down the Zeke over the field. Three or four Helldivers fired at the Sally, which had a brief charmed life, escaping the dive bombers only to be shot down by a fighter a few minutes later. It was nearly impossible to determine the extent of the damage done, but on departing from the first attack the squadrons saw four or five large columns of smoke from airplanes set on fire in bombing and strafing attacks. There were few Japanese aircraft in the air around the field. A VF-8 Hellcat quickly shot down a Tony that tried to intercept VB-8 Helldivers on their retirement. VF-8 also claimed a Nate, a Betty (likely the Sally that the Helldivers had fired on), and an Emily flying boat shot down northeast of Clark Field which may have been the same aircraft claimed by VF-31.

A fighter sweep preceded the second strike on Clark Field. Four Hellcats from VF-8 joined 12 from VF-31 and nine from VF(N)-41 making their second sweep over the airfields around Clark. VF-31's Hellcats were each carrying one 500lb bomb. Circling the field and seeing no enemy aircraft, the VF(N)41 and VF-8 divisions remained above as high cover while VF-31 went down to bomb the field. Only six aircraft bombed the field as the other six VF-31 Hellcats now reported Japanese aircraft approaching. In a running air battle over the Clark Field area and as the Hellcats made their withdrawal, VF-31 claimed 13 Japanese fighters shot down, including eight Tonys. This gave VF-31 29 claims for the day. The pilots later commented that the Japanese pilots failed to use teamwork in their attacks against the Hellcats, making individual attacks allowing the VF-31 divisions to always maintain numerical superiority.

The second strike against Clark Field in the afternoon that followed the fighter sweep was a repeat of the earlier effort. While the weather over the field had improved, smoke and haze limited observation of the results of the attack. The Helldivers of both air groups went in first, aiming for buildings and hangars around the airfield, getting hits, and starting fires, followed by the Avengers of the two torpedo squadrons. There were some hits on parked aircraft, the pilots reporting seeing 50–100 aircraft scattered around the field. On retiring, the crews could see three columns of smoke from burning aircraft. The escorting fighters had several combats, VF-18 claiming five Tonys shot down over the Clark Field area and VF-8 claiming two more and an Oscar.

Task Group 38.2's second strike of the day, and its first against shipping, was an attack on a convoy reported off the west coast of Luzon, near Capones Island northwest of Subic Bay. CVG-8 sent out 16 Hellcats to provide cover, ten Helldivers, and eight Avengers, while CVG-18 also launched 16 Hellcats and 15 Helldivers with eight Avengers. The convoy consisted of five merchant vessels with six escorts. The formation crossed the coast with the fighters above. The two Helldiver squadrons attacked first, while the torpedo squadrons circled around to prepare their attack. The ten VB-8 seriously damaged two Fox Baker freighters, a Fox Tare Charlie, and claimed to have sunk a Sugar Baker freighter with five near misses. Antiaircraft fire from the escorts hit the last SB2C to make an attack, sending the Helldiver down to crash into the water. VB-18 followed quickly, also claiming two Fox Bakers, a Fox

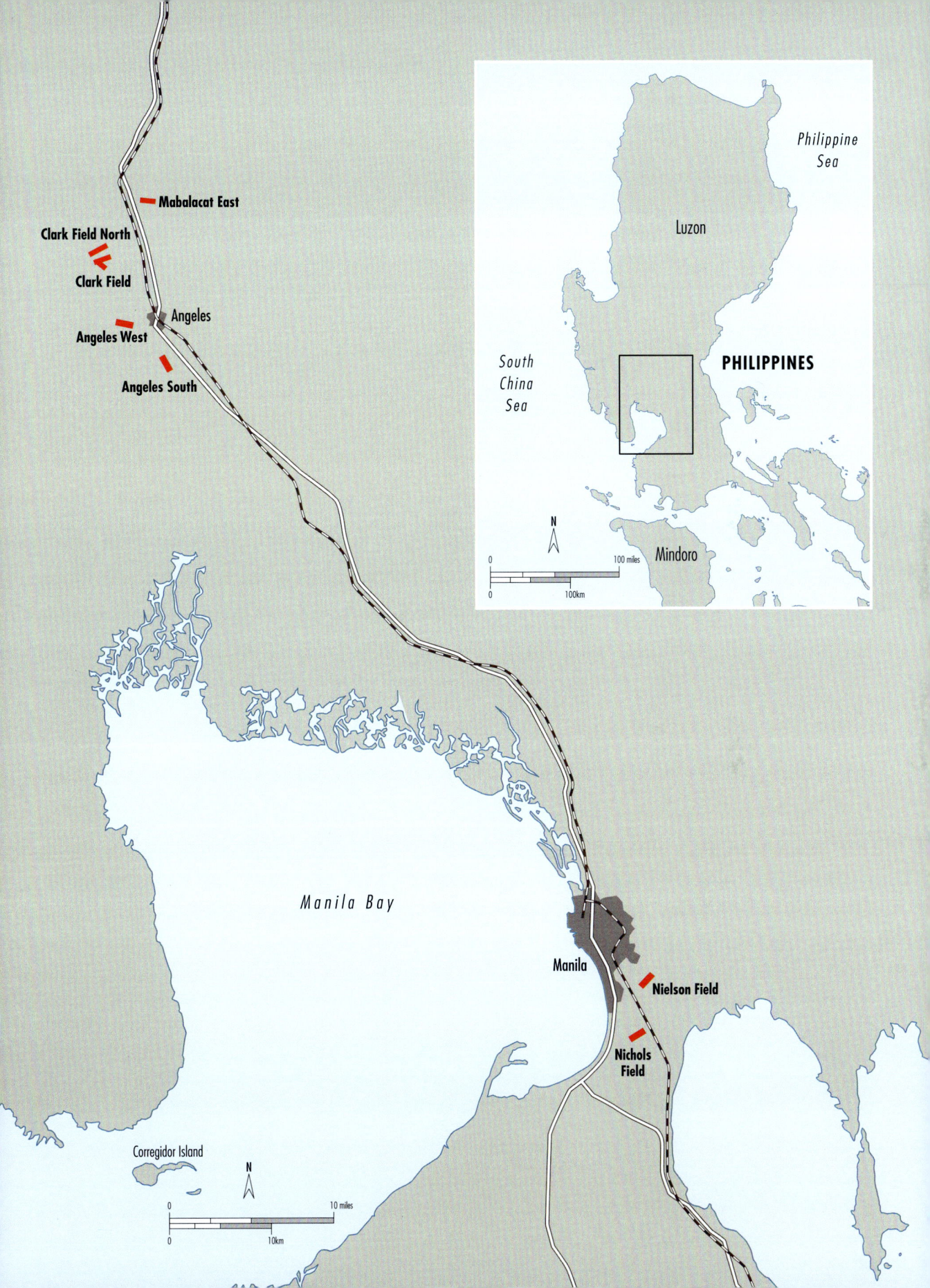

Able freighter, and two Destroyer Escorts seriously damaged. VT-18 began its torpedo runs after the dive bombers had finished their attacks, claiming one Fox Able freighter sunk with two torpedoes, a Sugar Able tanker sunk with one torpedo hit, and a Fox Baker freighter sunk with one torpedo as well, obtaining hits on two more Fox Baker freighters. VT-8 then came in for its attack. Four TBMs launched their torpedoes against a Fox Baker freighter, claiming it as sunk, while three launched their torpedoes against a Sugar Baker with unobserved results. Both torpedo squadrons recognized that they were likely to have duplicated their claims.

The two fighter squadrons both scored well against Japanese aircraft. Escorting the bombers on the return, VF-8 saw 25 Japanese aircraft taking off from the airfield at San Marcelino, northwest of Subic Bay, and sent down two divisions to attack. The Hellcats found a mixed group of Nates, Oscars, and Val dive bombers whose inexperienced pilots stood little chance. The pilots submitted claims for 13 aircraft destroyed, two probably destroyed, and seven damaged. After the air combat ended, several pilots went down to strafe the airfield, claiming an additional three aircraft destroyed and 15 damaged on the ground. VF-18 saw three Nates over Subic Bay apparently intent on intercepting the bombers and promptly shot down two. On the return flight from the attack on the convoy VF-18 pilots saw many aircraft over the Clark Field area and engaged in combat with numerous Tonys, claiming ten shot down. The Hellcat pilots found several bombers as well, claiming six Bettys and a single Helen (Ki-49) shot down.

On the last strike of the day CVG-8 and CVG-18 went after another convoy reported off the west coast of Luzon near the town of Santa Cruz. This convoy was comprised of eight freighters of different sizes, but the results were not as good as in the earlier shipping strike. VB-8 and VT-8 attacked with bombs getting only one hit on a freighter and several near misses, doing some damage. VB-18 had better luck, claiming one Fox Baker freighter sunk after seven SB2Cs dropped 1,000lb semi-armor piercing bombs on the ship, and two small freighters possibly sunk. For this mission VT-8's TBMs carried 2,000lb bombs, but could only claim damage to one large freighter. The escorting fighters had a relatively uneventful mission, VF-18 claiming one Val shot down. Antiaircraft fire hit one of the squadron's Hellcats causing the right aileron to jam in the up position. The pilot made it back to the task group where he made a successful water landing.

Like Task Group 38.2, Task Group 38.3 hit airfields and shipping in its four strikes on September 21. On the first strike CVG-15 hit Nichols Field and nearby Las Pinas airfield, while CVG-19 went after Nielson Field and adjacent airfields. Las Pinas appeared to be unused, so the attack focused on Nichols. VF-15's Hellcats carried 5" HVAR and fired off 36 at buildings around the field, while the dive and torpedo bombers hit other buildings and hangars with a combination of 1,000lb and 500lb bombs. On this mission VB-15 employed "window" to interrupt Japanese radar-guided antiaircraft guns. Just before entering a dive, the rear gunner would start throwing window out of the rear cockpit, throwing a bundle out every five seconds. The antiaircraft fire over Nichols was intense, but inaccurate, possibly due to the window.

During CVG-19's attack on Nielson Field, VF-19 claimed one Tony and one Zeke shot down, the only aircraft they could find airborne over the airfield. The Hellcats went down to strafe aircraft on Nielson claiming two Dinahs, a Zeke, a Topsy, and three Tojos destroyed with several more aircraft damaged. The Hellcats strafed a nearby airfield and claimed a Tony and a Topsy destroyed. The Helldivers and Avengers bombed hangars and buildings around the field, the Avengers dropping 350lb depth charges and claiming two Tabby transports (L2D) destroyed.

The two air groups returned to their respective targets for their second strikes. On this mission VF-15 carried 350lb depth charges which they used against buildings, hangars, and some of the estimated 75 aircraft parked around Nichols Field. The Helldivers of VB-15 claimed to have destroyed five or six aircraft through bombing, probably destroying an additional six aircraft. VB-19 hit Nielson Field again claiming 12 aircraft destroyed with bombs, and damage to more hangars and buildings. CVG-19 returned to the area for its third strike of the day in the early afternoon following a fighter sweep by the CVLG groups, with VF-22 and VF-27 joining VF-32, with VF-27 claiming a Sally bomber and VF-32 shooting down two Tonys and damaging a third. In its third strike, CVG-19 bombed Zablan and Quezon airfields near Nielson Field. VB-19 used window to divert the antiaircraft guns and was rewarded to see the explosions falling behind their aircraft. In this strike CVG-19 claimed eight aircraft destroyed.

CVG-15 carried out two strikes against shipping off the west coast of Luzon, with CVG-19 joining the final strike of the day. The targets were ships spotted along the coast north of Subic Bay, possibly survivors of the convoy attacked earlier in the day. In the first attack eight VF-15 Hellcats bombed what they identified as a destroyer with depth charges, believing the vessel was probably sunk. VB-15 attacked two Fox Tare Charlie freighters causing serious damage to both. For the first time in combat, VT-15 carried torpedoes, claiming one freighter sunk. The final strike of the day was an effort to finish off the ships attacked earlier. VB-15 claimed to have sunk two freighters, while VF-15 claimed heavy damage to two escort vessels with 5" rockets and strafing. VB-19 also claimed two freighters sunk with several direct hits, and a small freighter which exploded after several Helldivers strafed the ship with their 20mm cannon and started a large fire. A VF-19 pilot claimed a Frances shot down during this fourth strike for the last claim of the day.

So ended a day of widespread destruction. The CVG and CVLG squadrons submitted claims for 147 Japanese aircraft shot down, 16 probably shot down, and 33 damaged, as well as a substantial number destroyed or damaged on the ground. Invariably, in the heat of combat there were overlapping claims for aircraft shot down and destroyed on the ground. The main airfields – Clark, Nichols, and Nielson Fields – were hit hard with extensive damage to buildings and hangars, but several small airfields were hit as well. The attacks on Japanese shipping had gone well, though, as will be seen, the actual number of ships sunk in the attacks was less than claimed at the time. Task Group 38.1 claimed 16 freighters, a large oiler and two destroyers sunk in Manila Bay, with Task Group 38.2 claiming five, and Task Group 38.3 five merchant vessels and a destroyer sunk off Luzon's west coast.

The Japanese were hit hard, though not as hard as the initial Task Force 38 claims suggested. During the day, the 201st Air Group sent up 42 Zeros to intercept the attacking carrier aircraft, losing at least 20. By one estimate the Imperial Navy lost 44 aircraft on September 21, though whether this total includes aircraft destroyed on the ground is unclear. The two Japanese Army fighter regiments flying the Tony suffered as well. In its first engagement with American fighters, the 17th Fighter Regiment lost ten officers killed, while the 19th Fighter Regiment also lost ten pilots including the Regiment's Executive Officer. It is likely that more fighters were lost in combat with the pilots able to bail out. By the end of the next day of combat the 31st Fighter Regiment would be reduced to just

The carrier air groups returned to Manila on September 22 to bomb installations in the harbor. This photo shows oil barges going up in flames alongside Pier 7 in the harbor. (Air Group 15 Action Report for September 22, 1944, RG38, NARA)

six serviceable aircraft. Neither the Japanese Army nor the Navy could afford the loss of experienced pilots as overall pilot quality continued an inexorable decline. The attacks on the airfields disrupted preparations for the *Sho* operation, while damage to shipping played havoc with already tight shipping schedules and the growing shortage of transports for vital supplies and raw materials.

Admiral Halsey wanted Task Force 38 to carry out four more strikes against shipping and the Manila airfields on September 22 to add to the destruction of the previous day, but the approach of a possible typhoon forced him to cancel the last two strikes. Before the Task Force could launch its first fighter sweep and strike, a small force of Japanese aircraft attacked Task Group 38.1 through clouds and rain squalls. The Combined Fleet's operational policy of preserving the Japanese Navy's strength for the decisive battle meant, as one Navy admiral expressed in his diary, "in the end all its planes will be annihilated on the ground … If the planes are to be expended anyway, attack the enemy and perish!" Apparently the First Air Fleet agreed and decided to launch an attack on Task Force 38, though the few airplanes it could muster could do little. Early in the morning of September 22, two Irving night fighters on reconnaissance located the Task Force 160 miles from Manila. Six Judy dive bombers (D4Y) with an escort of nine Zeros from the 201st Air Group went out to attack Task Force 38.

Beginning at 0508hrs radar in several Task Force 38 ships began picking up bogies approaching. At 0527hrs the *Hornet* scrambled two F6F-5N night fighters from the VF(N)-76 detachment while the *Intrepid* sent off two night fighters from VF(N)-78. The VF(N)-78 fighters claimed a Zeke shot down and another damaged. The *Hornet* fighters shooting down a second shortly thereafter. One of the destroyers in Task Group 38.2 shot down an unidentified airplane which was seen to crash. Despite these bogies approaching, the carriers launched the first fighter sweeps and the first strikes around 0630hrs. At 0712hrs, taking advantage of clouds and rain, six Japanese aircraft avoided the CAP that had been launched and penetrated the screen of Task Group 38.1, dropping three bombs and strafing the *Hornet* and the *Monterey*, damaging four aircraft preparing for the next strike and wounding two men who later died of their wounds. Antiaircraft fire from the surrounding ships shot down three of the attackers and damaged two more, the attackers losing six aircraft to night fighters and the guns of the Task Force. Another attempt to attack the American carriers later that day had to be canceled when they could not be located.

On September 22, CVG-8 and CVG-18 went back to attack shipping off the west coast of Luzon. A photo taken from a VT-8 Avenger shows several freighters burning after attacks. (80G-281092, RG80, NARA)

The task groups made seven strikes against shipping in Manila Bay and the Manila dock area, and two strikes against ships that had been found the day before off the west coast of Luzon. There were fewer ships in the bay as many had apparently slipped out during the night. The first strike involved aircraft from the *Hornet*'s CVG-2, *Wasp*'s CVG-14, and *Essex*'s CVG-15, combining fighters, dive bombers, and torpedo bombers in coordinated attacks. It was hard for the pilots to distinguish ships that had not been hit in previous attacks. Targets were scarce, but the bombers went in and claimed several large and medium-size freighters sunk or seriously damaged. As the formation flew west over Manila Bay, a formation of Tonys came near, but the escorting fighters from VF-2 and the fighter bombers from VB-2 kept them away. On the second strike, aircraft from CVG-19 on the *Lexington* and from CVLG-28 on the *Monterey* also participated. On this strike CVG-15 and CVG-19 concentrated on hitting piers, buildings, warehouses, and oil storage tanks, doing considerable damage but not enough to incapacitate the harbor. As the bombers completed their dives a group of eight to ten Tonys tried again to intercept. VF-15 claimed one as a probable, but VF-19 got more involved fighting them off, claiming six Tonys destroyed, with two probables and a damaged, with VF-2 claiming two more destroyed. This was close to the number of Tonys actually lost. The 19th Fighter Regiment sent up seven Tonys to intercept the attacking carrier airplanes, losing six fighters to the escorting Hellcats.

A group of young Japanese Navy pilot trainees in Japan. By early 1944, the quality of flight and combat training in the Japanese Army and Navy had begun an inexorable decline that only worsened as the war went on. (Author's collection)

On their second strike of the morning the *Intrepid*'s CVG-8 and *Bunker Hill*'s CVG-18 went looking for shipping along the west coast of Luzon south of San Fernando, the scene of attacks on convoys the day before. Several of the ships hit during the strike had been hit before, but the air groups claimed severe damage to several ships and a few sunk. CVG-18 found several freighters to the north that did not appear to have been attacked before, claiming one medium and one small freighter sunk and a third probably sunk. The escorting fighters from VF-18 found a group of Pete floatplane fighters (F1M) on the north shore of San Fernando Bay and claimed five destroyed.

The airfield strikes concentrated on Clark Field and the fields nearby, and Nielson Field near Manila. Just before the first strikes on Clark Field, VF-31 from the *Cabot* and VF(N)-41 off the *Independence*, with several fighters from VF-18, carried out a fighter sweep over the area. Seeing no enemy aircraft in the air, the two squadrons went down to bomb and strafe aircraft and buildings on the field. VF(N)-41 claimed four twin-engine aircraft destroyed at Clark and six more destroyed at nearby Angeles West field. The two squadrons then flew on to reconnoiter Lingayen airfield, at the bottom of Lingayen Gulf, but en route saw a flight of six Val dive bombers. Both squadrons attacked, VF-31 claiming six Vals shot down while VF(N)-41 claimed three from the same formation, clearly a case of over-claiming, and an escorting Zeke fighter.

CVG-8 and CVG-18 attacked Clark Field and Angeles West on their first strike of the day. The dive and torpedo bombers hit buildings and parked aircraft around the fields claiming seven aircraft destroyed and 21 damaged at Clark Field and 12 destroyed at Angeles West, including five Tonys from either the 17th or 19th Fighter Regiment. VF-18 lost one Hellcat to antiaircraft fire over Clark Field. At the same time, CVG-19 with CVLG-32 hit Nielson Field bombing buildings, hangars, and barracks around the field. The dive bombers claimed ten aircraft destroyed on the ground, while VT-19 dropped 500lb bombs

Attacks on shipping off Panay Island

The final strikes on targets in the Philippines, on September 24, 1944, concentrated on Japanese shipping. Having searched for shipping around Cebu and Negros, VB-8 and VT-8 headed north and found three Japanese freighters cruising off the east coast of Panay using several islands as cover. The Helldivers of VB-8 dropped 1,000lb bombs on the Japanese ships in dive bombing attacks, strafing the ships with their 20mm cannon in their dives. Coming in after the dive bombers, the Avengers of VT-8 dropped 2,000lb and 100lb bombs in glide bombing attacks. The squadrons claimed to have sunk one 7,000 ton and one 2,000 ton freighter and to have severely damaged a third 4,000 ton freighter, without damage to any of the attacking aircraft.

Japanese shipping in Coron Bay, Busuanga Island, seen off the wing of a VB-18 Helldiver. The shipping in Coron Bay was the main target for Task Force 38's last strikes on the Philippines. The Japanese had believed that Coron Bay was beyond the range of American aircraft, but in one of the longest carrier strikes of the war to date, Task Force 38's Helldivers and Hellcats carried out a successful attack. (Carrier Air Group 18 Action Report for September 24, 1944, RG38, NARA)

among 10–12 twin-engine aircraft, claiming five destroyed. VF-32 bombed buildings and the runway area at Nielson as well, then flew west on a sweep over Manila Bay where the squadron saw a Sally bomber flying below, promptly shooting it down. The squadron flew on to Subic Bay finding several small ships at the mouth of the bay and went down to strafe. Antiaircraft fire from the ships hit one of the Hellcats, which fortunately made a water landing beyond the bay where the pilot was rescued by an American submarine.

For the rest of the day the task groups sent out strikes across the Visayas looking for aircraft and shipping around Cebu, Leyte, Negros, and Panay. There were few aircraft to be found in the air or on the ground. By the end of the day the air groups had submitted claims for just seven aircraft shot down over the Visayas with additional claims for 28 aircraft destroyed on the ground at nine different airfields. The strike missions found shipping scattered around the Visayas, hitting ships near Panay, in between Cebu and Leyte, off Masbate, and in Cebu harbor, where the bombers hit dock installations again. The air groups claimed more freighters and smaller craft sunk and damaged, and one Imperial Navy minesweeper sunk northeast of Panay.

With the weather worsening as a typhoon approached, Admiral Halsey called off the afternoon strikes. The carriers recovered airplanes from the second strikes and Task Force 38 headed southeast towards a refueling rendezvous. Early that evening one of the destroyers from Task Group 38.3's screen picked up a pilot and crewman from an SB2C from the *Intrepid*'s VB-18 who had been shot down on September 12 during the strikes on the Visayas.

Over the two days of strikes against Manila, Task Force 38's air groups flew 1,398 sorties, split nearly equally between strikes on the airfields and on shipping. The aircraft claimed destroyed on the second day were an indication of how successful the first day's air combat and airfield strikes had been. On September 22 the air groups submitted claims for just 26 Japanese aircraft shot down, with three more probables and three damaged. For the full two days of strikes the air groups claimed 173 Japanese aircraft shot down (contemporary reports state the figure as 169), with 188 destroyed on the ground. Task Force 38 estimated that there were approximately 65 ships in the area, almost all merchant vessels. Of these, the air groups claimed to have sunk 34, probably sunk eight, and damaged a further 23. Task Force 38's losses were 11 fighters and fighter bombers, three dive bombers, and two torpedo bombers, fewer than lost during the strikes on the Visayas and a loss rate of 1.1 percent of the total sorties flown. There were additional aircraft that had been damaged in air combat that could not be repaired on board. By now the flow of replacement aircraft was so ample that damaged aircraft could simply be pushed over the side. Thirteen pilots and aircrew were killed in action. Operational losses amounted to three fighters and two torpedo bombers. Neither combat nor operational losses were over just yet.

The second strike on the Visayas, September 24, 1944

Admiral Halsey had received Intelligence that the Japanese were holding some of the ships that had escaped Manila and others plying the main shipping route to Japan at Coron Bay on Busuanga Island, located between Mindoro and Palawan, until the American carriers had withdrawn from the Philippines. This natural harbor was thought to be beyond the range of American carrier aircraft, as it was located over 300 miles from Samar, the most likely approach point for the carriers. Admiral Halsey ordered his three task groups to prepare for a long-range strike against shipping in Coron Bay on September 24, and to also plan for three more strikes against targets in the Visayas.

For the strike on shipping in Coron Bay, Task Force 38 decided to send only F6F Hellcats, some armed with bombs, and SB2C Helldivers. The strike force was to consist of 96 Hellcats, with 72 carrying one 500lb bomb each, and 72 Helldivers. Each task group was ordered to furnish 32 fighters and 24 dive bombers, with the CVLG groups providing the fighter escort. As this was a long-range mission, one of the longest missions the Fast Carrier Task Force had yet attempted, all the Hellcats carried centerline drop tanks and the Helldivers were fitted with two 58-gallon wing tanks. After refueling on September 23, the task groups left the fueling area some 200 miles east of Samar Island and by early morning had arrived at a point 50 miles northwest of Samar, where the carriers began launching their planes a little after 0600hrs.

The Carrier Air Group commander from CVG-8 led the strike and acted as target evaluator. While nearing the island of Mindoro on the way to Coron Bay, two naval vessels opened fire on the strike force. The strike force leader directed the *Wasp* and *Hornet* air groups from Task Group 38.1 to attack these and several other naval vessels

With the attack underway several Japanese ships can be seen smoking in Coron Bay. The Hellcats and Helldivers made repeated runs over the ships in the bay. (Carrier Air Group 18 Action Report for September 24, 1944, RG38, NARA)

Attack on shipping at Coron Bay

Cabilauan Island

EVENTS

1. **0600hrs.** The strike force, comprising 96 Hellcats and 72 Helldivers, launches from their carriers and after rendezvous heads nearly due West towards Busuanga Island. Mechanical problems force several aircraft to land back aboard. Enroute to the target area the CO of Air Group 8, acting as Target Evaluator, directs Task Group 38.1's VB-2, VB-14, and VF-14 to attack three Japanese naval vessels at the southern tip of Mindoro.

2. **0730–0800hrs.** VB-8, leading Task Group 38.2 squadrons, approaches Busuanga Island. The target evaluator sights six merchant ships off the northern coast of the island, near Cabilauan Island, fourteen merchant ships off the southern coast of Busuanga in Lusong Bay between Lusong Island and Sangat Island, and several more ships to the west near Marily Island.

3. **0800–0830hrs.** The target evaluator directs Task Group 38.2 squadrons to attack the ships in the Lusong Bay area and tells three Task Group 38.3 squadrons (VB-15, VF-15, and VB-19) to attack the ships off the northern coast near Cabilauan Island. Task Group 38.3's two other squadrons, VF-27 and VF-32, head for ships sighted off Coron Island.

4. **0845hrs.** VB-8 and VB-18 make the first attacks on the ships in Lusong Bay, bombing at masthead height with 1,000lb. bombs. VF-31 and VF(N)-41 follow with glide bombing and strafing attacks on ships to the west off Marily Island.

5. **0930hrs.** VF-27 and VF-32 make masthead-level attacks on several ships off Coron Island dropping 500lb. bombs.

6. **0830hrs.** VB-15 and VB-19 dive bomb the ships on the northern side of the island, dropping 1,000lb. bombs. VF-15 Hellcats make repeated strafing runs against the ships to silence antiaircraft fire. F6F Hellcat fighter bombers from Task Group 38.1's VB-2 join in the attack. Two VB-2 Hellcats fly south to strafe ships in Coron Bay.

7. After completing their attacks, the squadrons make for the rendezvous point and return to their carriers between 1100hrs and 1145hrs, having flown more than five hours.

A remarkable photograph showing a VB-18 Helldiver on a glide bombing approach toward a Japanese freighter. The Helldiver's bomb bay doors are open and drop tanks for added range can just be seen under the wings. (Carrier Air Group 18 Action Report for September 24, 1944, RG38, NARA)

A view of Coron Bay from a departing Helldiver. Numerous Japanese ships are now on fire. Post-war analysis confirmed that the strikes sank 13 Japanese merchant ships and six Japanese naval vessels. (Carrier Air Group 18 Action Report for September 24, 1944, RG38, NARA)

seen off the southern tip of Mindoro while leading the rest of the force on to Coron Bay. VF-8 and VB-8 were first to arrive in the target area, with VB-18 and 32 Hellcats from VF-31 and VF(N)-41, seeing 12 large and medium freighters in Lusong Bay, at the northwest end of Coron Bay, and another six freighters on the north side of Busuanga Island opposite Coron Bay. Task Group 38.2 attacked the ships in Lusong Bay. VB-8 attacked first using, for the first time, masthead bombing where the SB2Cs released their bombs, fitted with a 4–5 second delay fuse, at an altitude of 200ft. On the way to the target, four of the squadron's SB2Cs had to abort the mission due to problems with their drop tanks, leaving five to make the attack. Four of the Helldivers attacked a Fox Tare Charlie freighter at the southern end of Lusong Bay, getting several near misses while the fifth Helldiver attacked a larger Sugar Able freighter claiming one direct hit.

Over the next hour the other air groups from Task Group 38.2 and 38.3 made attacks on shipping around Coron Bay and Busuanga Island. VB-18 also used the masthead bombing technique, strafing ships on the approach and releasing the first of two 500lb bombs at 150ft, coming in on a second run to release the second bomb. The squadron made a third run to strafe the ships they had attacked through intense antiaircraft fire which claimed one of the SB2Cs, the pilot making a successful water landing. VB-18's Helldivers claimed hits on nine freighters and believed they had left six ships sinking and two more seriously damaged, but lost two more Helldivers on the return flight to the Task Group, probably from running out of fuel.

VF-31 and VF(N)-41 flew as escorts to the Task Group 38.2 strike force, each squadron sending out 16 Hellcats, with eight armed with 500lb bombs. Seeing no enemy aircraft above the ships, the squadrons kept eight airplanes up as high cover over the strike while the bomb-carrying Hellcats came down to attack ships in Lusong Bay. The Hellcats dropped their bombs at masthead height, strafing on their bomb runs, and returning to make repeated passes over ships around the bay. Each squadron claimed one freighter sunk and damaged several others. One of VF(N)-41's pilots saw what he thought was a small fast vessel speeding to the southeast, but then the wake stopped and the "boat" continued on. He realized it was a Japanese seaplane. Closing quickly he identified the airplane as a Jake twin-float reconnaissance seaplane and shot it down.

Task Group 38.3 attacked the group of six ships on the north coast of Busuanga Island, with CVG's VB-19 accompanying VF-15 and VB-15 from CVG-15, as well as VF-32 off the *Langley* and VF-27 off *Princeton* flying as escort with some Hellcats carrying 500lb bombs. VB-15 and VB-19 apparently used standard dive bombing tactics, dropping their bombs on several freighters without observing the results. One of VF-32's divisions joined in this attack, bombing from masthead height and claiming damage to several ships. The other divisions joined VF-27 in attacking ships in Lusong Bay and achieved several hits on three freighters as well as strafing several small escort vessels.

While the other air groups were attacking the merchant vessels around Coron Bay, CVG-14 from the *Wasp* and CVG-2 from *Hornet* went after the naval vessels reported off the southern tip of Mindoro. Their attacks illustrate the difficulties even experienced Navy pilots had in identifying their targets and the damage done to them. VB-14 had sent ten SB2C-3 and eight F6F-3 fighter bombers on the strike, with an escort of eight Hellcats from VF-14. Crossing the southern tip of Mindoro above an overcast, the strike force saw some explosions of antiaircraft fire, and located several naval vessels through a hole in the overcast which they identified as an Imperial Navy cruiser and a destroyer escort. Eight SB2Cs and seven of the F6Fs attacked the ship identified as a cruiser, claiming two direct hits and several near misses, strafing the ship during the bomb runs, and leaving it smoking and dead in the water. The destroyer escort was also bombed and strafed and pilots saw it explode and sink. After completing the attack the strike force rendezvoused and went after a reported destroyer found off the east coast of Mindoro. Identifying this ship as a Chidori-class torpedo boat, the Helldivers and Hellcats made repeated strafing runs causing an explosion and seeing the ship sink. This was in fact the Ōtori-class torpedo boat *Hayabusa* which was sunk on this date at this location.

Postwar analysis of Imperial Navy ship losses identified the larger ship not as a cruiser, but the substantially smaller minelayer *Yaeyama* that was in company with Subchasers No. 32 and No. 39, not a destroyer escort. Correctly identifying the vessel as a minelayer but seeing no apparent damage, eight SB2C-3s from VB-2 attacked and got two direct hits, possibly just before VB-14's attack, leaving the minelayer listing and leaking oil. It appears that VB-14 did destroy the two subchasers nearby. VB-2's eight F6F-5 fighter bombers then flew on to Coron Bay where they attacked a freighter and an oiler, claiming severe damage to both.

The strike forces had an uneventful return to their task groups, having seen only one Japanese aircraft airborne during the attacks on Coron Bay and around Mindoro and flying back in perfect weather. It had been, for almost all the pilots, the longest carrier strike they had ever attempted. Some of the Hellcat pilots had been in the air for over six hours.

By early evening all the strike aircraft had returned to their carriers and the task groups turned away from the Philippines heading to anchorages for rest and replenishment. Task Group 38.1 went to Manus in the Admiralties, Task Group 38.2 to Saipan, and Task Group 38.3 to Kossol Passage at the north end of the Palau Islands where Task Group 38.4 was still covering the invasion forces. Task Force 38 had concluded the carrier strikes on the Philippines with a remarkable bag of 365 Japanese aircraft shot down, four more shot down by the ships of the Task Force, and 511 destroyed on the ground for a total of 880 aircraft. The claims for shipping were equally impressive, with 149 ships claimed sunk, 56 more probably destroyed, and 94 damaged. Damage to ground installations at airfields and harbors was extensive. Task Force 38's own losses amounted to 54 aircraft lost in combat with, sadly, 59 pilots and aircrewmen killed or missing in action.

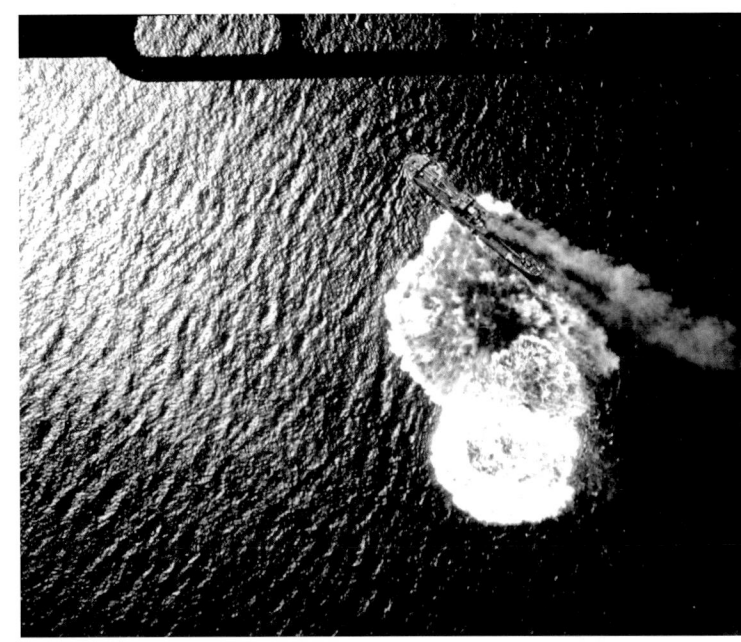

During the day other air groups searched for Japanese shipping around other islands in the Visayas. CVLG-32 off USS *Langley* (CVL-27) found several ships near Masbate, west of Samar and attacked this freighter. The air group claimed four ships sunk and a further ten probably sunk over the course of the day. (80G-281083, RG80, NARA)

ANALYSIS AND CONCLUSION

As well as attacks on shipping, the air groups made several final strikes against the Japanese airfields on Negros. Here a Japanese twin-engine aircraft, possibly damaged in an earlier attack, burns after a strafing attack by CVG-14 off USS *Wasp* (CV-18). (Task Group 38.1, Report On Strikes Against the Visayas, September 24, 1944, RG38, NARA)

The carrier strikes across the Philippines during September 1944 were a demonstration of the immense power contained in the US Navy's Fast Carrier Task Force. The strikes took place at a time when American power, and the industrial capacity that lay behind it, was not just in the ascendence over Japan but overwhelmingly so. None of Task Force 38's six fleet carriers and seven light carriers, nor much of the Task Force's screen or the supporting fleet train, had been built before the war. The majority of pilots who carried out the strikes had been trained after the attack on Pearl Harbor. They flew a new generation of carrier aircraft that also had come into service after the Pearl Harbor attack and that were, in most cases, superior to similar types of Japanese aircraft. The combination of the quantity and quality of materiel available to Task Force 38, together with capable leadership at all levels of command, made possible the first extended assault by a force of aircraft carriers against a large land mass and land-based air power.

Task Force 38 successfully completed its mission of inflicting maximum attrition on Japanese forces, though for reasons related to Japanese plans for the *Sho* operation, the strikes did not draw out the Japanese fleet as Admiral Nimitz had hoped. The carrier strikes did inflict severe damage to Japanese air power in the Philippines, though less than claimed at the time. The figure of 880 Japanese aircraft destroyed in the air and on the ground was several multiples greater than the total number of aircraft the Japanese Army and Navy had available. The majority of aircraft claimed destroyed in the air were single-engine fighters, predominantly the Zero, Oscar, Nate, and Tony. Task Force 38's air groups claimed approximately 93 Zeros, 57 Oscars, 25 Nates, and a remarkable 81 Tonys, three times the number actually lost. There were comparatively fewer claims for twin-engine aircraft. Some types, like the Dinah, Frances, and Irving, were shot down while searching for Task Force 38, while the ten Nick fighters of the 45th Fighter Regiment claimed were attempting to intercept the carrier aircraft striking their airfields. Other types were bombers and transports who appeared not to have received warning of the carrier strikes. While precise numbers are hard to determine, it appears that the Japanese Navy lost over 100 aircraft in the air and on

An important outcome of the September Strikes was the conclusion that fighter bombers could replace the SB2C dive bombers on Essex-class carriers. After January 1945 the Navy added a squadron of fighter bombers to each Essex-class carrier. Here a VBF-84 F4U-1D takes off from USS *Bunker Hill* (CV-17) in March 1945. (80G-312614, RG80, NARA)

the ground while the Japanese Army lost 55–60 aircraft in the air alone. By the end of the strikes the Navy's First Air Fleet had just 25 Zero fighters and 38 other aircraft available in the Philippines.

The carrier strikes against Japanese aircraft and airfields in the Philippines took place as the Japanese Army and Navy were near to completing their preparations for the *Sho* operation and the expected American invasion of the islands. Neither service could afford the loss of experienced aircrew and ground staff, the destruction of airfield installations, and the disruption of training. An unforeseen outcome of the carrier strikes was a hasty reinforcement of Japanese air power in the Philippines. The Japanese Navy rebuilt its air units so that by early October the Navy had some 230 aircraft in the Philippines, of which 149 were serviceable, including 81 Zeros in the 201st Air Group. The Japanese Army rushed the 16th Air Brigade (16th Hikōdan) to the Philippines with the 51st and 52nd Fighter Regiments equipped with the new Nakajima Ki-84 Type 4 Fighter ("Frank") and the 26th and 204th Fighter Regiments with the Ki-43 Oscar, joining the re-equipped 17th, 19th, 30th, and 31st Fighter Regiments. More units were alerted for movement to the Philippines when the *Sho* operation was activated.

As with the claims for Japanese aircraft, with multiple aircraft attacking the same target it is not surprising that claims for Japanese shipping exceeded the number actually lost. A detailed postwar analysis of Japanese naval and merchant shipping losses determined that during the September carrier strikes Task Force 38's aircraft sank 55 merchant vessels and 12 naval vessels, around 45 percent of the number of ships claimed to have been sunk. However, the damage done was still considerable. The greatest shipping losses were from the attacks on shipping in Manila and off the coast of Luzon, which cost the Japanese 25 merchant ships and three naval vessels, followed by the attacks on September 24 which saw 13 merchant ships and six Navy ships lost. The attacks on shipping in Manila and Coron Bay cost the Japanese 19 merchant ships of greater than 5,000 tons displacement. The main prize was sinking four large 10,000 ton tankers which Japan could ill-afford. At Coron Bay the Imperial Navy lost the 9,000 ton seaplane tender *Akitsushima*, the largest Navy vessel lost during the carrier strikes.

It is again important to point out that it was not just ships sunk that caused damage. Every ship that was sunk, every damaged ship that needed repair, every dock and harbor facility destroyed or damaged had a ripple effect throughout the Japanese military and civilian logistics systems. These attacks all across the Pacific and Southeast Asia disrupted shipping schedules and reduced carrying capacity, causing delays in deliveries of critical equipment, supplies, food, and raw materials. A lack of parts might keep an airplane on the ground where it would be subject to destruction through air attack, lack of fuel would limit both operational flying and flying training, and delays in getting raw materials would slow production in Japan and the replacement of lost ships and aircraft. The destruction Task Force 38 inflicted on Japanese forces in the Philippines therefore had a wider effect, helping to maximize attrition on the entire Japanese war economy.

It can be argued that the September carrier strikes on the Philippines set the stage for later attacks on Formosa (as Taiwan was then called), the Philippines in support of the landings on Leyte, the invasion of Okinawa in proximity to the Japanese Home Islands, and attacks on the Home Islands themselves. The main conclusion the US Navy drew from the September carrier strikes was the demonstration of the power of carrier-based air power against Japanese land-based air power. As a confidential report stated a few weeks after the carrier strikes on the Philippines:

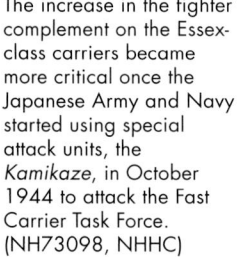

The increase in the fighter complement on the Essex-class carriers became more critical once the Japanese Army and Navy started using special attack units, the *Kamikaze*, in October 1944 to attack the Fast Carrier Task Force. (NH73098, NHHC)

In this instance we were not attacking a series of isolated air bases; we were challenging an air force deployed in depth over a system of many coordinated airfields. While not defended as the home Empire will be, the Philippines had all the potentiality of a major land-based air force. And yet it collapsed like a house of cards. At times air opposition was extremely sharp, and yet it never seems to have developed into a major threat against the carriers themselves. The lesson should not be pushed too far, and it certainly does not prove that a carrier air force can function with impunity against any land-based force. But it does appear to demonstrate that it can function with considerable confidence against anything that the Japs can throw at it.

It is ironic that this report appeared just a few weeks before the Japanese unleashed a powerful new weapon, the *Kamikaze*, that presented the Fast Carrier Task Force with a dangerous new threat.

The second conclusion that came out of the September carrier strikes was the realization that if the Fast Carrier Task Force was to go up against land-based air power in the future, particularly against the Japanese homeland, the carriers had to be able to establish and maintain air superiority over the target areas as well as over the fleet. Establishing air superiority required fighter aircraft, and many of them. In his report on the September carrier strikes, Vice Admiral Marc Mitscher wrote: "Particularly in attacks against the Japanese mainland, it is problematical whether our present fighter strength is sufficient to maintain control of the air over the target area and still provide adequate defense for the carrier task groups."

Mitscher wanted more carriers in the task forces, and more fighters per carrier. The answer was to reduce the number of dive bombers or torpedo bombers and to replace them with fighter bombers. He argued that since the most effective weapon against ships was the torpedo, the carriers should retain the TBM. During the September strikes on the Philippines, CVG-2 and CVG-14 had demonstrated that the F6F Hellcat was a good dive bomber and good low-level bomber, and superior to the TBM or SB2C in firing rockets. The F4U Corsair was equally as good, and faster than the F6F. Reducing the number of dive bombers on the large fleet carriers and replacing them with either the F6F or the F4U in the fighter bomber role would not reduce a carrier's offensive power. With proper training, fighter bomber pilots could be used just as well as fighters. Mitscher recommended that the future composition of air groups on the fleet carriers should be one torpedo bomber squadron with the TBM, one fighter bomber squadron with either the F6F or F4U, and two fighter squadrons with either the F6F or the F4U.

The arrival of the *Kamikaze* over the Philippines accelerated changes in air group composition. By November the fighter squadrons on the fleet carriers had 50–54 fighters assigned, with a reduction in the dive bomber complement to 24 SB2Cs. After January 1945 the fighter complement on the fleet carriers was increased to 72 fighters and the dive bombers cut back to 15. The increase in fighters came from adding Marine Corps F4U squadrons to the carriers as well as adding more F6Fs and F4Us to existing fighter squadrons. When this became too many aircraft and pilots for one squadron to manage, the Navy split the squadron in two, re-designating one squadron as a fighter bomber squadron (VBF), each with 36 fighter aircraft. The dive bomber squadrons remained on the fleet carriers but now with 15 SB2Cs with the torpedo squadrons equipped with 15 TBMs. With this new complement of aircraft the Fast Carrier Task Force, reverting to Task Force 58 under Admiral Spruance and Vice Admiral Mitscher, supported the invasion of Okinawa with attacks on the Japanese homeland. Part way through the battle for Okinawa, Task Force 58 became Task Force 38, again when Admiral Halsey and Vice Admiral McCain replaced Spruance and Mitscher, leading the Fast Carrier Task Force in extended attacks against the Japanese Home Islands until the end of the war.

FURTHER READING

Buell, Harold L., *Dauntless Helldivers: A Dive-Bomber Pilot's Epic Story of Carrier Battles* (Orion Books, 1991)
Clark, Adm. J.J. USN (Rtd), with Clark G. Reynolds, *Carrier Admiral* (David McKay Company, 1967)
Davis, William E., *Sinking the Rising Sun: Dog Fighting & Dive Bombing in World War II* (Zenith Press, 2007)
Faltum, Andrew, *The Essex Aircraft Carriers* (Nautical & Aviation Publishing Company, 1996)
Faltum, Andrew, *The Independence Light Aircraft Carriers* (Nautical & Aviation Publishing Company, 2002)
Fisher, Stan, *Sustaining the Carrier War: The Deployment of U.S. Naval Air Power in the Pacific* (Naval Institute Press, 2023)
Halsey, Admiral William F. and Lt Cdr J. Bryan, III, *Admiral Halsey's Story* (McGraw-Hill Book Company, 1947)
Hargreaves, Lt Cdr Everett C., *Son of a Preacher: A Hellcat Ace's Memoirs* (BAC Publishers, 2003)
Hata, Ikuhiko, Yasuho Izawa, and Christopher Shores, *Japanese Army Air Force Fighter Units and their Aces 1931–1945* (Grub Street, 2002)
Hata, Ikuhiko, Yasuho Izawa, and Christopher Shores, *Japanese Naval Air Force Fighter Units and their Aces 1932–1945* (Grub Street, 2011)
Hearn, Chester G., *Carriers in Combat: The Air War at Sea* (Praeger, 2005)
Hone, Trent, *Mastering the Art of Command: Admiral Chester W. Nimitz and Victory in the Pacific* (Naval Institute Press, 2022)
Houston, Charles, *Flying with the Iron Angels: Carrier Air Group Fourteen and the USS Wasp CV-18* (Charles Houston, 2001)
Japanese Monograph Series No. 12, *Philippines Air Operations Record (Army) 1944–1945*
Japanese Monograph Series No. 82, *Philippine Area Naval Operations, Part I (Air): Jan.–Sept. 1944*
Matloff, Maurice, *United States Army in World War II: The War Department: Strategic Planning for Coalition Warfare 1943–1944* (USGPO, 1959)
Morrison, Samuel Eliot, *History of the United States Naval Operations in World War II: Volume VIII: New Guinea and the Marianas March 1944–August 1944* (Little, Brown and Company, 1953)
Morrison, Samuel Eliot, *History of the United States Naval Operations in World War II: Volume XII: Leyte June 1944–January 1945* (Little, Brown and Company, 1958)
Potter, E.B., *Nimitz* (Naval Institute Press, 1976)
Potter, E.B., *Bull Halsey* (Naval Institute Press, 1988)
Reynolds, G. Clark, *The Fast Carriers: The Forging of an Air Navy* (McGraw-Hill Book Company, 1968)
Sherman, Admiral Frederick C., *Combat Command: The American Aircraft Carriers in the Pacific War* (E.P. Dutton, 1950)
Swope, Robert Jr., *Tall Dogs & Hellcats: A History of Air Group Two* (Heritage Trails, 2002)
Taylor, Theodore, *The Magnificent Mitscher* (W.W. Norton & Company, 1954)
Tillman, Barrett, *Hellcat: The F6F in World War II* (Naval Institute Press, 1979)
Trimble, William F., *Admiral John S. McCain and the Triumph of Naval Air Power* (Naval Institute Press, 2019)
Vego, Milan, *The Battle for Leyte, 1944: Allied and Japanese Plans, Preparations, and Execution* (Naval Institute Press, 2006)
Winters, Captain T. Hugh, *Skipper: Confessions of a Fighter Squadron Commander 1943–1944* (Champlin Fighter Museum Press, 1985)

INDEX

References to images are in **bold**.

Admiralty Islands 5, 15–16
air crew:
    Japanese 37–38
    US 26–27
aircraft, Japanese 28–29, 33–35, 36–37
    Ki-45 Nick 63, **64–65**
    and losses 90–91
    and Luzon 70
aircraft, US 93, 45–46
    Boeing B-29; 6
    F6F Hellcats 16, 17, **23**, **26**, 63, **64–65**
    SB2C Helldivers **9**, 16, 17–18
    TBF/TBM Avengers **11**, 18–19
    Vought OS2U Kingfishers **51**
airfields, Japanese 23, 25, **30**, 32–33
Akitsushima (seaplane tender) 92
Aleutian Islands 5
Angaur 40
Arbes, Lt Cdr J. D. 71
Arnold, Cdr Jackson 13
Arnold, Gen 66
Australia 6, 7

Bacolod 29, 32, 44, 60, 61, 62
Barnes, USS 68
Belleau Wood, USS 50, 63, 67, 68, 69
Biak 5–6
Bogan, Rear Adm Gerald 13
Bohol 52
bracketing 25–26
Bulan 52, 53
Bunker Hill, USS 13, 17, 71, 81, **91**
    and Mindanao 51, 52
    and Visayas 53, 60–61
Cabot, USS 49–50, 51, 52, 70
    and Visayas 60–61, **63**
Caroline Islands 5, 15–16
Carrier Air Groups (CAGs) **14**, 16
carriers, US 13–16
Cebu 52–56, 61, 84
Celebes 41, 68
Chichi Jima 45, 46
China 7, 43
Clark, Rear Adm J. J. "Jocko" 12
Clark Field 29, 32, 69, 70
    and strikes 71, **72–73**, 75–76, 78, 79, 81
concentration 25

Core, USS 13
Coron Bay **84**, 85, **86–87**, 88–89, 92
Cowpens, USS **15**, 68, 70
    and Mindanao 49, **50**, 67

Davison, Rear Adm Ralph 12–13
disposition 25
dive bombing 20, 22, 25
Doyle, Capt Austin 13

Eniwetok 15–16
Enterprise, USS 11, 13, 17, 45, 46
Espiritu Santo (New Hebrides) 15–16
Essex, USS **9**, 13, **14**, 17
    and Luzon 80
    and Mindanao 47, 48
    and Visayas 63, 66–67
Essex-class carriers 13–14, 15, 16

Fabrica 61–62
Fast Carrier Task Force 4, 6
    and aircraft 17–19
    and CAGs **14**, 16
    and carriers 13–16
    and targets and tactics 19–20, **21**, 22–23, **24**, 25–26
    and Task Force 58 6, 11
    see also Task Force 38
formations 19, **20**
Formosa (Taiwan) 6, 8, 43, 92
Franklin, USS 17, 45–46
Fujimoto Katsumi, Lt 63

Germany 7, 8
Gilbert Islands 5, 7
glide bombing 22, **24**, 25
Great Britain 7, 66
Greer, Capt Marshall 13
Grumman 17
Guadalcanal 5, 11
Guam 15–16

Haggerty, Lt (jg) C. J. **23**
Haha Jima 46
Halmahera 41
Halsey, Adm William 5, 7, 11–12, 45, 93
    and Luzon 69, 80, 84
    and Mindanao 48
    and objectives 41, 43
    and Visayas 52, 53, 66, 67, 68, 85
hangars 23, 25
Hayabusa (torpedo boat) 89

Hirohito, Emperor 29
Hollandia **4**, 5
Home Islands 6, 92, 93
Hornet, USS 13, 16, 17, 56
    and Coron Bay 85, 88, 89
    and Luzon 74, 80
    and Mindanao 49–50

IJA *see* Imperial Japanese Army (IJA)
IJN *see* Imperial Japanese Navy (IJN)
Imperial General Headquarters (IGHQ) 6, 32, 43, 44
Imperial Japanese Army (IJA) 4, 5, 6, 91
    and air units 28–29
    and bases and facilities 32–33
    and Luzon 70, 79–80
    and objectives 43–44
    and order of battle 39
    and supplies 19–20
    and targets and tactics 36–37
Imperial Japanese Navy (IJN) 4, 5, 6, 39
    and air crew 37–38
    and air units 29, 31
    and bases 32–33
    and Luzon 70, 79–80
    and objectives 43–44
    and shipping losses 91–92
    and supplies 19–20
    and targets and tactics 36–37
Independence, USS 70
Independence-class carriers 13, 14–15, 16
Intrepid, USS 17, 60–61, **67**
    and Luzon 80, 81, 84
    and Mindanao 51, 52
Iwo Jima 45–46

Japan defences 5–6
Joint Chiefs of Staff (JCS) 4–5, 7–8, 66

Kamikaze **92**, 93
King, Adm Ernest J. 8, 11, 12, 66
Kurile Islands 6

Langley, USS 48, 63, 70, 88
Leahy, Adm William **7**, 66
Legaspi 36, 60–61
Lexington, USS 17, 47, 81
    and Visayas 63, 66–67
Leyte 5, 8, 66
    and landings 92
    and strikes 52, 53
Landing Ship, Tanks (LSTs) **4**

INDEX

Luzon 8, 36
   and airfields 32
   and railroad 20
   and strikes 68–71, **72–73**, 74–76, 78–81, 84–85
Landing Vehicles Tracked (LVTs) **5**, **40**

MacArthur, Gen Douglas 7, 8, 40–41, 66
McCain, Vice Adm John 12, 93
McCampbell, Cdr David 13, 47, 48, 60
Mactan Island 54, 55, 56, 60
Malaya 4
Manila 68, 69
   and airfields **77**
   and strikes **71**, 74–75, **79**, 80–81, 92
Marianas Islands 4, 5, 6, 17
   and Turkey Shoot (1944) 27
marksmanship 25
Marshall, Gen 66
Marshall Islands 5
Mindanao 5, 8
   and airfields 31, 40–41, 43
   and reconnaissance 36
   and strikes 47–52, 67
Mindoro 85, 88, 89
Mitscher, Vice Adm Marc 11, 12, 93
Monnosuke Ono, Col 29
Monterey, USS 69, 70, 80, 81
Morotai 8, 40–41, 43, 68–69

Nassau, USS 13
Negros 29, **31**, 32, **90**
   and strikes 52–53, 54, 56–57, **58–59**, 60, 61–63, **64–65**, 66–67
Netherlands East Indies 6, 7
neutralization 23
New Britain *see* Rabaul
New Guinea **4**, 5, 7
Nichols Field 32, **68**, 69–70, 71, 78–79
Nielson Field 69–70, 71, 74, 78–79, 81, 84
Nimitz, Adm Chester 7, 8, 11, 13, 90
   and Luzon 69
   and objectives 41, 43
   and Visayas 66
Nishi Susumu, Maj 29

Okinawa 92, 93
operations:
   A-Go (1944) 5, 6
   Sho-Go (1944) 6

Sho Operation No. 1 (1944) 43–44, 52
Stalemate II (1944) 40
Tradewind (1944) 41

Palau Islands 8, 40, 43, 66
Panay 52–53, 66–67, 81, **82–83**, 84
Pearl Harbor 14, 15, 26–27, 90
Peleliu 40, 41
Philippine Sea, Battle of the (1944) 6
pilots:
   Japanese 37–38, **81**
   US **19**, 26–27
position 25
Prince of Wales, HMS 4
Princeton, USS 48, 49, 63, 70, 88

Rabaul 5, 7
radar 33, 49
reconnaissance 17, 36
recruitment 26–27
Repulse, HMS 4
Rigg, Lt Cdr James **47**
Roosevelt, Franklin 7, 14
Ryukyu Islands 6

Saipan **5**, 6
Samar 52, 53
San Jacinto, USS 45, 46
Saratoga, USS 13
Satsuki (destroyer) 75
Sherman, Rear Adm Frederick C. 12
Shipley, Cdr Ralph 13
shipping, Japanese 91–92
Solomon Islands 5, 7, 11
Spruance, Adm Raymond 11, 12, 93
strafing tactics 20, **21**, 23
Sunosaki (repair ship) 75

tactics:
   Japanese 36–37
   US 19–20, **21**, 22–23, **24**, 25–26, 27
Taiwan *see* Formosa (Taiwan)
targets:
   Japanese 36–37
   US 19–20, **21**, 22–23, **24**, 25–26
Task Force 38; 5, **9**, 15
   and air groups 18
   and carrier strikes **42**
   and commanders 11–13, **14**
   and crew 26–27
   and Luzon 69–71, 74–76, 78–81, 84–85
   and Mindanao 41, 43, 47–52
   and Morotai 68–69
   and preliminary actions 45–46
   and Visayas 53–57, **58–59**, 60–63, 66–68, 85, 88–89
Teraoka Kinpei, Vice Adm 31
Thach, Lt Cdr John 26
Tojo Hideki, Gen 6, 29
Tominaga Kyoji, Lt Gen 29
torpedo attacks 22–23, 25, 74–75
Toyoda Soemu, Adm 29
training:
   Japanese 29, 32
   US 27, 37–38
Truk 5

Ulithi Atoll 15–16, 41, 45, 46
US Marine Corps **5**, 93
US Naval Academy 12, 13, 26
US Navy:
   and objectives 40–41, 43
   and order of battle 38–39
   see also Fast Carrier Task Force

Visayas 32, 84
   and first strikes 52–57, **58–59**, 60–63, **64–65**, 66–68
   and second strikes 85, **86–87**, 88–89
Vogelkop Peninsula 40–41

War Plan Orange 6, 7
Washington, USS **16**
Wasp, USS 13, 16, 17, **27**
   and Coron Bay 85, 88, 89
   and Luzon 74, 80
   and Mindanao 49–50
   and preliminary action 46
   and torpedoes **47**
weaponry, Japanese 33–35, **44**
   cannons 37
   machine guns 46
weaponry, US 14, 17–19
   bombing 20, 22, **24**, 25
   HVAR rockets 11
   torpedoes 22–23, 25, 74–75
Weller, Capt Oscar 13
White Plains, USS 13

Yaeyama (minelayer) 89
Yap 41, 45, 46
Yorktown, USS 12